Revise IGCSE

Complete Study & Revision Guide

Byron Dawson and Ian Honeysett

Biology

FOUNDATION® BOOKS

Contents

1 Characteristics and classification of living organisms

2 Organisation and maintenance of the organism

3 Development of the organism and the continuity of life

4 Relationships of organisms with one another and with their environment

Preparing for the examination

Planning your study

The final three months before taking your IGCSE examination are very important in achieving your best grade. However, the success can be assisted by an organised approach throughout the course.

- After completing a topic in school or college, go through the topic again in your Revise IGCSE Biology Study Guide. Copy out the main points again on a sheet of paper or use a highlighter pen to emphasise them.
- A couple of days later, try to write out these key points from memory. Check differences between what you wrote originally and what you wrote later.
- If you have written your notes on a piece of paper, keep this for revision later.
- Try some questions in the book and check your answers.
- Decide whether you have fully mastered the topic and write down any weakness you think you have.

Preparing a revision programme

At least three months before the final examination, go through the list of topics in your Examination Board's specification. Go through and identify which topics you feel you need to concentrate on. It is a temptation at this time to spend valuable revision time on the things you already know and can do. It makes you feel good but it does not move you forward.

When you feel you have mastered all the topics, spend time trying past questions. Each time check your answers with the answers given. In the final couple of weeks go back to your summary sheets (or highlighting in the book).

How this book will help you

Revise IGCSE Biology Study Guide will help you because:

- it contains all the **essential content** for your IGCSE course without the extra material that will not be examined
- it contains **Progress Checks** and **IGCSE questions** to help you confirm your understanding
- it gives **sample IGCSE questions** and advice from an examiner on how to improve
- the summary table will give you a **quick reference** to the requirements for your examination
- **marginal comments** and **highlighted key points** will draw to your attention towards important things you might otherwise miss.

Five ways to improve your grade.

1. Read the questions carefully

Many students fail to answer the actual question set. Perhaps they misread the question or answer a similar question they have been set before. Read the question once right through and then again more slowly. Some students underline or highlight key words in the question as they read it through. Questions at IGCSE contain a lot of information. You should be concerned if you are not using the information in your answer.

2. Give enough detail

If a part of a question is worth three marks, you should make at least three separate points. Be careful that you do not make the same point three times. Approximately 25% of the marks on your final examination papers are awarded for questions requiring longer answers.

3. Quality of Written Communication (QWC)

From 2003 some marks on the IGCSE papers are given for the quality of your written communication. This includes correct sentence structures, correct sequencing of events and use of scientific words.
Read your answer through slowly before moving on to the next part.

4. Correct use of scientific language

There is important scientific vocabulary that you should use. Try to use the correct biological terms in your answers and spell them correctly. The way biology language is used is often a difference between successful and unsuccessful students. As you revise, make a list of the biological terms that you meet and check that you understand the meaning of these words.

5. Show your working

All biology papers include some calculations. You should always show your working in full. Then if you make an arithmetical mistake, you may still receive marks for correct biology. Check that your answer is given to the correct number of significant figures and give the correct unit.

Characteristics and classification of living organisms

The following topics are covered in this section:

● *Characteristics, classification and diversity of living organisms*
● *Adaptations of organisms to their environment*
● *Use of simple keys in classification*

What you should know already

Complete the following passages using words from the list. You may use the words more than once.

cell membrane   cells   chloroplasts   fertilise   nucleus   photosynthesis   respiration
sensitivity   seven   sperm   swim   tail   waste   specialised

All organisms are made up of units called 1._____. These units are surrounded by a 2._____
which controls what enters and leaves the cell. The 3._____ is the control centre of the cell. Plant cells
contain 4._____ that make food by 5._____.

The diagram shows a type of animal cell.

Most cells are 6._____ for the job that they perform. The diagram above illustrates a 7._____ cell.
The job of this cell is to join with or 8._____ an ovum. To help it do this, it has a 9._____ so that
it can 10._____ towards the ovum.

Living organisms are different from non-living material because they carry out 11._____ vital processes.
These are often called characteristics of living organisms. The ability to respond to changes occurring around
them is called 12._____. Excretion is the ability to remove 13._____ products that have been
produced by the organism. The release of energy from food molecules is called 14._____.

ANSWERS

1. cells; 2. cell membrane; 3. nucleus; 4. chloroplasts; 5. photosynthesis;
6. specialised; 7. sperm; 8. fertilise; 9. tail; 10. swim; 11. seven; 12. sensitivity;
13 waste; 14. respiration

1.1 Characteristics of living organisms

After studying this chapter you should be able to:

- *list the various characteristics of living organisms*
- *characterise the various systems of living organisms*
- *define and understand various terms related to living organisms. Nutrition, excretion, respiration, sensitivity, reproduction, growth.*

MRS Gren

M: Movement   In response to changes

R: Respiration   Breaking down of food in cells to release energy

S: Sensitivity   Ability to sense and respond to changes in its surrounding

G: Growth   An increase in size, mass, complexity of an organism

R: Reproduction   Producing offspring similar to the parent

E: Excretion   Removal of waste products made by chemical reactions inside the cell

N: Nutrition   Feeding / obtaining nutrients for growth, energy and maintenance of good health.

Respiration and breathing are different

Faeces is not an example of excretion; because it is not formed through metabolic process.

Some non-living things may show one or two of these characteristics but living things show all the seven above mentioned characteristics.

 PROGRESS CHECK

1. Which living characteristic is exhibited by an earthworm when it moves away from light?
2. a. A fresh bean seed before soaking water weighs X gm. After soaking it, it weighs Y gm. Can this change in weight be termed as "growth"?
   b. Ten days later the seed germinates and looks like a young seedling, but still weighs only Y gm. Can this change be called growth? Justify your answer.

3. Study the list of things shown below and decide whether you think they are living, were once living but are now dead, or are non-living:

Light bulb	Apple
Paper bag	Mushroom
Sand	Coal
Spider	Glass jar
Woollen sweater	Rose
Copper jug	Bathroom sponge

An example, **rubber**, has been solved for you.

Item	Living	Non-living but once part of a living thing	Non-living and never part of a living thing
Rubber		✔	
Light bulb			
Paper bag			
Sand			
Spider			
Woollen sweater			
Copper jug			
Apple			
Mushroom			
Coal			
Glass jar			
Rose			
Bathroom sponge			

PROGRESS CHECK

4. The following list shows ten non-living things which were once a part of a living thing:

Leather	Cardboard
Petrol	Silk
Butter	Wool
Ivory statue	Cooking oil
Wine	Pearl

Which living things do these items originate from?
What change has occured in each item since the time it was part of a living thing?

An example, **rubber**, has been solved for you.

Name of the item	Original living thing	How it has been changed
Rubber	Rubber tree	Rubber tapped from the tree is moulded into a certain shape.
Leather		
Petrol		
Butter		
Ivory statue		
Wine		
Cardboard		
Silk		
Wool		
Cooking oil		
Pearl		

PROGRESS CHECK

PROGRESS CHECK

1. Sensitivity

2. a) No, because the seed has absorbed water but the number of cells remain the same.
   b) Yes, because the seed has grown into a seedling which means that the division of cells has happened.

3. Rubber – Non-living but once part of a living thing;
   Light bulb – Non-living and never part of a living thing;
   Paper bag – Non-living but once part of a living thing;
   Sand – Non-living and never part of a living thing;
   Spider – Living;
   Woollen sweater – Non-living but once part of a living thing;
   Copper jug – Non-living and never part of a living thing;
   Apple – Living;
   Mushroom – Living;
   Coal – Non-living but once part of a living thing;
   Glass jar – Non-living and never part of a living thing;
   Rose – Living;
   Bathroom sponge – Non-living and never part of a living thing;

4.

Name of the item	Original living thing	How it has been changed
Rubber	Rubber tree	Rubber tapped from the tree is moulded into a certain shape.
Leather	Animal skin	Skin of dead animals is removed; it is cleaned and moulded into articles.
Petrol	Parts of animals	Parts of animals, buried under high temperature and pressure change into petroleum.
Butter	Milk	Butter is churned out of milk.
Ivory statue	Animal tusk	Elephant's tusk removed and carved.
Wine	Grapes	Fermented grapes.
Cardboard	Plants	Paper formed from plants is made into cardboard.
Silk	Silk worms	Silk worms form threads to make their cocoon which is removed to weave silk.
Wool	Animals' hair or fur	Hair or fur is removed from the outer part of animals like sheep and woven into threads.
Cooking oil	Seeds	Mustard and sesame seeds are ground to produce oil.
Pearl	Molluscs	Formed inside the shell of molluscs.

1.2 Classification and diversity of living organisms

LEARNING SUMMARY

After studying this section you should be able to:

- *explain the principles of a modern classification system*
- *describe how organisms are scientifically named*
- *understand the five-kingdom classification system*
- *describe the characteristics of the five kingdoms and realise that it becomes sometimes difficult to differentiate between plants and animals*
- *describe the structure of viruses*
- *explain how viruses reproduce*
- *explain bacterial structure, function and its adaptative features*
- *understand the features of fungi*
- *explain the difference between monocotyledonous and dicotyledonous plants*
- *explain how invertebrates are classified*
- *identify animals with the help of visible characteristic features of Arthropods, Annelids, Nematodes, Crustaceans, Arachnids, Myriapods, Molluscs, Insects*
- *make simple dichotomous keys to identify organisms.*

KEY POINT

Scientists have carried out the process of classifying organisms into groups for a long time. This chapter looks at the modern systems of classification and sees that these methods, besides being convenient, tell us a lot about the evolution of organisms.

Principles of classification

Artificial versus natural classification

Humans have been classifying organisms into groups ever since they started studying them. This makes it much more convenient while trying to identify an unknown organism.

KEY POINT

The systematic arrangement of organisms on the basis of their interrelationship is called taxonomy.

This classification system means that very different organisms end up in the same group.

The system that was used for a long time used one characteristic to classify a group of organisms. For example:

Classification of vertebrates

Vertebrates – are the animals with a definite back bone or vertebral column. They include:

1. **pisces (fish)**

    Presence of fins, gills, scales and showing external fertilisation

2. **amphibians**

    They live both in water and on land, have two pairs of limbs, moist skin without scales. Their larvae have tails and gills and they undergo metamorphosis

3. **reptiles**

    They bear dry scaly skin, two pairs of pentadactyle limbs. Their eggs are laid with yolk and shell

4. **aves (birds)**

    Body covered with feathers, forelimbs modified into wings, beaks for feeding, eggs are laid

5. **mammals**

    Skin covered with hair, two pairs of pentadactyle limbs, respiration through lungs, give birth to babies, suckle their young

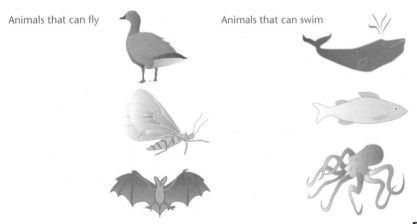

Animals that can fly   Animals that can swim

Fig. 1.1

This type of system is called an artificial system.

In the 17th and 18th centuries John Ray and Carl Linnaeus developed a new system. This system puts organisms that share the most common characteristics together in groups.

The advantage of this type of system is that organisms that are in the same group are more likely to have evolved from the same ancestors.

> **KEY POINT** This system is used today and is called the Natural System. The old system was called the artificial system.

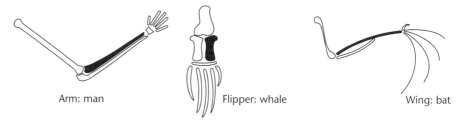

| Arm: man | Flipper: whale | Wing: bat |

Similarity in fore limb structure   **Fig. 1.2**

A natural system classifies man, whales and bats in the same group because although their limbs do different jobs, they are all similar in structure and share other similarities.

> **KEY POINT** Organisms are put into the same species if they can breed with each other to produce fertile offspring. So species is the basis for classification and evolution.

Naming organisms

Linnaeus also introduced a universal system for naming organisms. This saved a lot of confusion because organisms had previously had different names in different countries or areas.

> **KEY POINT** The system Linnaeus introduced is called the Binomial system.

Each organism has two names in Latin, the first is the name of the genus and the second the species, for example:

Binomial name of human is *Homo sapiens*.

Here *Homo* is the name of genus and *sapiens* is the name of species.

Advantages of classification:

a.   Makes study of wide variety of organisms systematic and easier.

b.   Gives a clear picture of how each organism is related to other one.

The binomial name is always in italics when typed. The genus starts with a capital letter but the species does not.

Fig. 1.3

Grouping and naming

Linnaeus introduced a system of smaller and smaller groups into which organisms are placed. Kingdoms are the largest groups and species the smallest groups. The smaller the groups, the more similar the organisms. For example, a lion is classified as follows:

Remember:

Peas

Carrots

Onions

For

Good

Soup

Kingdom	Animalia	–	animals
Phylum	Vertebrata	–	animals with backbones
Class	Mammalia	–	warmblooded animals with hair or fur, suckle young
Order	Carnivora	–	flesh eating mammals
Family	Felidae	–	cats, large and small
Genus	*Panthera*	–	certain large cats, such as tigers and panthers
Species	*leo*	–	lion only

To decide if organisms are similar enough to be in the same species seems obvious but some members of the same species look quite different.

PROGRESS CHECK

1. Which is the correct binomial name for man:
   (a) *Human being*   (b) *homo sapiens*   (c) *Homo Sapiens*   (d) *Homo sapiens*
2. Why do some members of a species look different compared to others?
3. A horse and a donkey can breed to produce an infertile animal called a mule. Are horses and donkeys members of the same species?

1. (d);   2. There is variation in all populations;   individuals change to adapt to their environment;   3. No, had they been from the same species, the offspring would have been fertile.

1.2.1 Concept and use of a classificatory system

The five kingdoms

How many kingdoms?

When classifying organisms, the first step is to place them in a kingdom. Most modern systems have five kingdoms.

> **KEY POINT** The five kingdoms are Bacteria, Fungi, Protoctista, Plants and Animals.

This system was suggested by the scientists Margulis and Schwartz.

The hardest job is often deciding whether an organism is an animal or a plant. The main difference is the way that they feed.

Plants make their own food by photosynthesis, but animals need ready-made food.

Fig. 1.4

Fig. 1.5

Diagram of protista (Amoeba)

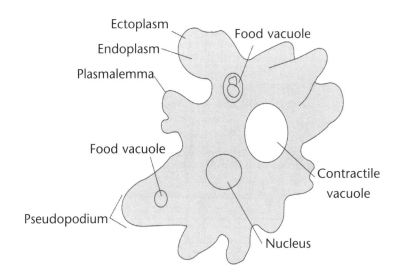

Ectoplasm

Food vacuole

Endoplasm

Plasmalemma

Food vacuole

Pseudopodium

Nucleus

Contractile vacuole

Fig. 1.6

Plants

Classification of plants is as follows:

There are four main phyla in the plant kingdom.

Kingdom–PLANTS
Have chlorophyll (green), cell walls contain cellulose

No roots; poor transport system (no xylem, phloem) | Presence of roots, stems and leaves, good transport system

Mosses
Simple leaves and stem, shed spores

Rhizoids

Ferns

Leaves in bud are coiled

Conifers
Cone-bearing trees and shrubs; seeds but no fruits, needle-like leaves

Flowering plants
Flowers from seeds within fruits

Class–Monocotyledons:
one seed-leaf. Strap-shaped leaves with parallel veins

Class–Dicotyledons:
two seed-leaves. Various-shaped leaves with main vein and others branching off

Fig. 1.7

Characteristics of monocot plants
- One cotyledon on their seeds
- They have long narrow leaves

e.g. corn, paddy, etc.

Characteristics of dicot plants
- Two cotyledons on their seeds
- They have broad leaves

e.g. gram, peas, etc.

Commonly found animals

Nematodes
1. Narrow, non-segmented bodies, round in cross section
2. Complete digestive tract
3. Most are free living but some are parasites and disease causing

e.g. round worm *Ascaris*

Annelids
1. Worm like animals with segmented bodies. Segments are visible as rings
2. Segments are separated by septa
3. Body is externally protected by a thin layer of cuticle

e.g. earth worm, leech

> The animal kingdom contains a number of phyla. Most commonly found animals belong to four phyla: Nematodes, Annelids, Arthropods and Mollusca.

Arthropods

1. Their body is covered with a thick chitinous cuticle, these animals show moulting.
2. They have compound eyes.
3. They possess adaptive features like spinnerets, poison glands, poison claws.
4. Sexes are separate.

e.g. grasshopper

Arthoropoda can be further divided into different groups like Insecta (mosquito, ant), Crustacea (prawn), Arachnida (spider) and Myriapoda (millipede, centipede).

Insects – Pairs of joint legs, pairs of wings.

e.g. grasshopper, butterfly, cockroach, etc.

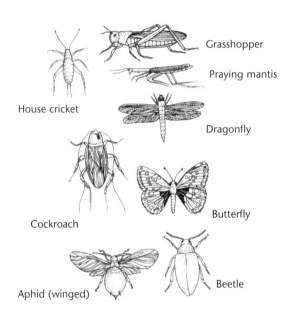

Common Insects – largest group of Arthropods   **Fig. 1.8**

Crustaceans – They have a pair of legs joint on each segment of the body.

e.g. prawn

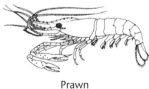

Prawn   **Fig. 1.9**

Arachnids – They have four pairs of limbs.

e.g. spider

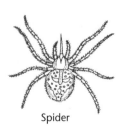

Spider   **Fig. 1.10**

Myriapods – They have pairs of legs on each body segment and one pair of antennae.

e.g. millipedes and centipedes.

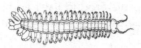

Centipede

Millipede

Fig. 1.11

Mollusca
1. Unsegmented, soft bodied animals.
2. They carry a shell formed by themselves on their bodies.
3. They have rasping tongue like radula.

e.g. snail, slugs.

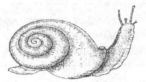

Land snail

Pila/Apple snail

Fig. 1.12

Bacteria, viruses and fungi

All these organisms belong to another group as they possess special characteristic features, due to which they cannot be placed into either plant or animal kingdom.

Bacteria

The kingdom containing the simplest organisms includes all bacteria. They vary in size and shape but are all single cells. They are smaller than animal or plant cells with a simple internal structure.

- Bacteria are classified according to their shape.
- They are aerobic.
- They form a cyst or an endospore.
- They act as decomposers in the nutrient cycles.

A generalised bacterium

A micrometer (μm) is 0.001 of a mm. Animal cells are often 30 μm across.

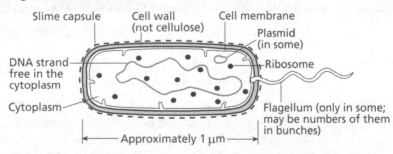

Slime capsule   Cell wall (not cellulose)   Cell membrane
Plasmid (in some)
DNA strand free in the cytoplasm
Ribosome
Cytoplasm
Flagellum (only in some; may be numbers of them in bunches)
Approximately 1 μm

Fig. 1.13

KEY POINT Bacteria contain DNA in the cytoplasm, never the nucleus. Therefore they are known as prokaryotes.

Bacteria – Adaptations

1. Bacteria produces a slimy layer to protect itself.

2. It can form a capsule around itself and remains inactive for a very long period of time, till the unfavourable conditions are over. Then endospore is formed.

3. It reproduces both sexually and by binary fission.

4. It can grow literally in every habitat–water, air, soil, inside an organism.

> **Fungi lack chlorophyll and are heterotrophic.**
>
> **Some show symbiotic relationships.**

Fungi

Members of this kingdom share some of the properties of plants but unlike plants, they cannot make their own food.

 KEY POINT Fungi are made up of many tubes of cytoplasm called hyphae. They do not contain chlorophyll and although they have cell walls, they are not made of cellulose.

Two common types of fungi are moulds and yeast.

Fig. 1.14

> **Yeast is unlike most fungi because it is not made up of hyphae. It is made up of individual cells.**

Part of a mycelium from a mould

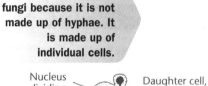
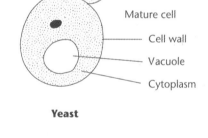

Nucleus dividing

Daughter cell, reproducing by budding

Mature cell

Cell wall

Vacuole

Cytoplasm

Yeast

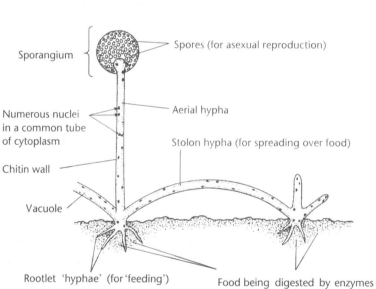

Sporangium — Spores (for asexual reproduction)

Numerous nuclei in a common tube of cytoplasm

Aerial hypha

Stolon hypha (for spreading over food)

Chitin wall

Vacuole

Rootlet 'hyphae' (for 'feeding')

Food being digested by enzymes

Fungi – Adaptations

1. It forms a hyphae which can grow and absorb nutrition from the organic matter.

2. Reproduction is through spore formation which can remain dormant until the favourable conditions are met.

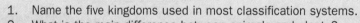

PROGRESS CHECK

1. Name the five kingdoms used in most classification systems.
2. What is the main difference between animals and plants?
3. Which main characteristics do fungi share with plants and which with animals?

1. Bacteria, protoctista, plants, animals and fungi; 2. The way in which they feed. Plants make their own food, whereas animals need ready-made food; 3. Fungi need ready-made food, like animals. They have a cell wall like plants although it is not made up of cellulose. Like plants they tend to respond slowly to stimuli and cannot move.

Viruses

Viruses are smaller than living cells, even bacteria.

> **KEY POINT** They consist of a protein coat, which surrounds a strand of genetic material. They are not cells.

Viral structure

A nanometer (nm) is a thousandth of a micrometer.

The genetic material is DNA in some viruses and RNA in others.

They are considered as the connection between living and non-living things.

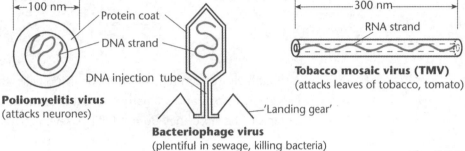

Poliomyelitis virus (attacks neurones)

Bacteriophage virus (plentiful in sewage, killing bacteria)

Tobacco mosaic virus (TMV) (attacks leaves of tobacco, tomato)

Fig. 1.15

Viruses bear the dual characters of living as well as non-living materials

Viruses are living because
- they have definite shape and morphology
- they have DNA/RNA
- all are parasitic and attach to a specific host.

Viruses are non-living because
- they can be crystallised
- they lack cellular structure and metabolism
- they lack respiration
- outside the host they are similar to chemical substances.

Virus – Adaptations

- Viruses are extremely small and do not contain the cellular structure; it is very easy for them to survive in the normal atmospheric conditions.
- They can reproduce in a specific host cell only.
- Due to their special structures like small size and the protein capsid, they are able to invade a bacterial cell.

Reproduction in viruses

Viruses need living cells in order to reproduce. In doing so they destroy the cell and so they are all parasites.

> **KEY POINT** Viruses inject their genetic material into the cell and take over the cell. They then use the cell's material to make new viruses.

The diagram shows how a virus attacks a bacterial cell.

'Life cycle' of a bacteriophage

Because viruses spend a lot of time inside the host's cells, this makes it difficult to kill them.

① Attachment

② Virus injects DNA (genes) into bacterium

③ Virus DNA replicates

④ Virus DNA 'orders' assembly of protein coat around DNA

⑤ Cell dies and bursts

⑥ New viruses liberated from dead cell to attack further bacteria

Fig. 1.16

Although viruses can reproduce inside living cells, they do not grow, feed, excrete or respire and so many scientists do not really recognise them as living organisms because they do not fulfil all seven characteristics of living things.

PROGRESS CHECK

1. How many times bigger is the generalised bacterium shown on page 17 compared to the poliomyelitis virus shown on page 19?
2. How does a virus take over a living cell?
3. Which characteristics of living organisms do viruses possibly show?
4. List the groups found in invertebrates.
5. Define taxonomy.
6. What are the characteristic features of nematodes?
7. How are bacteria classified?
8. Why are viruses considered non-living at times?
9. How do bacteria survive adverse conditions?

1. 10 times; 2. By injecting its genetic material; 3. They reproduce, and possibly show some movement and sensitivity.
4. Nematodes, Annelids, Arthropods, Molluscs, Echinoderms.
5. Systematic arrangement of organisms on the basis of their interrelationship is called taxonomy.
6. Narrow, non-segmented, bodies round in cross section, complete digestive tract; most are free living but some are parasites and disease causing.
7. Bacteria are classified according to their shape.
8. Because when they are outside the host cell they do not show characters of living things.
9. They form a cyst around themselves which protects them.

1.2.2 Dichotomous keys

Variations in organisms:
1. Structural – number of fingers, toes, etc.
2. Functional – male/female
3. Behavioural – timid/aggressive
4. Chemical – neurotransmitter
5. Other ways – blindness

Following dichotomous key can be used to reach a conclusion.

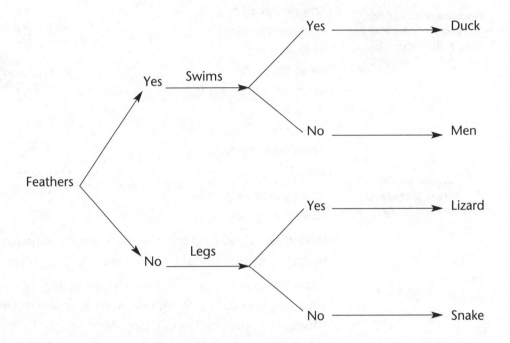

Arthropods – Adaptations

1. Body is segmented and is covered by an exoskeleton of protein and chitin to protect the inner body parts.

2. **Crustaceans** breathe through lungs, insects have tracheal system to breathe, spiders and scorpions have book lungs depending upon the environment they live in.

3. **Acrachnids**, e.g. spiders have spinnerets to spin a web, scorpions have poison glands to protect themselves.

4. Some **insects** have a life cycle during which they change their form known as **metamorphosis**.

5. **Myriapods** produce a calcareous shell which is used for protection.

Adaptation of insects

Insects are, in terms of numbers, the most successful organisms living on land. There are over 7,50,000 different species of insects. There are a number of reasons why they are so successful, but one is the variety of their feeding methods. They do not have jaws but they have a tremendous variety of mouthparts so that different species feed on different foods.

> **KEY POINT**
> The variety of insect feeding methods means that they are not all competing for the same type of food.

> Mosquitoes may inject parasites, such as the malaria parasite, when they feed.

An example of a specialised feeding method is the mosquito's. The mosquito penetrates the skin and injects a substance that stops the blood from clotting.

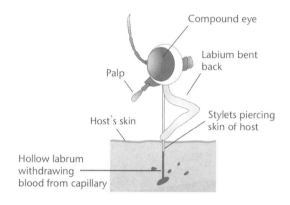

Compound eye

Labium bent back

Palp

Host's skin

Stylets piercing skin of host

Hollow labrum withdrawing blood from capillary

Fig. 1.17

> Aphids may also spread pathogens from plant to plant.

Aphids (greenflies) pierce plants to tap the food in the phloem.

Houseflies suck up food that they have partially digested with enzymes and butterflies suck up nectar from flowers.

Some insects undergo a complete change during their life. This means that the adult may feed on a different food from its offspring. This reduces competition between the adult and its offspring.

> **KEY POINT**
> This complete change in body form is called metamorphosis.

Fig. 1.18

> The adult lays eggs that hatch into larvae.

Larva (e.g. caterpillar)   Pupa (e.g. chrysalis)   Adult (e.g. butterfly)

Adaptations in plants

Adaptations develop over time and generations as a response to the ever changing environment. It allows an organism to reduce competition for space and nutrients, reduces predation and increases reproduction. There are, however, several factors that can limit these adaptations, e.g. availability of water, light, predation and temperature.

Desert plants have adapted to the extremities of heat and aridity by using both physical and behavioral mechanisms, much like desert animals.

Plants that have adapted by altering their physical structure are called **xerophytes**. Xerophytes, such as cacti, usually have special means of storing and conserving water. They often have few or no leaves, thus reducing the amount of transpiration.

Phreatophytes are plants that have adapted to arid environments by growing extremely long roots, that allow them to acquire moisture at or near the water table. The term, phreatophyte, literally means water-loving plant.

Plants and living on land

Plants cannot move around looking for water and so living on land presents them with problems. One problem is reproduction. In water, sex cells can swim to each other but on land this is more difficult. Flowering plants have developed pollen grains that contain the male gamete. It is often transferred to another plant by insects.

> **KEY POINT** Flowering plants are usually adapted for pollination by wind or insects.

The mass of the bee on the landing pad moves the anthers or the stigma so that they touch the bee's back.

More variation is produced by cross pollination.

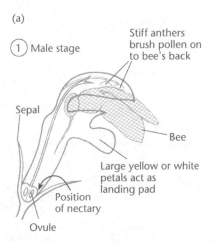
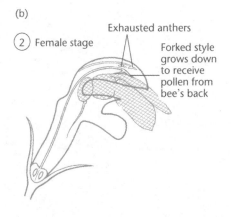

(a) ① Male stage — Stiff anthers brush pollen on to bee's back — Sepal — Bee — Large yellow or white petals act as landing pad — Position of nectary — Ovule

(b) ② Female stage — Exhausted anthers — Forked style grows down to receive pollen from bee's back

Fig. 1.19

The white deadnettle is pollinated by bees. The male parts of the plant ripen before the female parts. This stops the flower from pollinating itself.

Cacti live in some of the driest deserts and so have many adaptations to enable them to gain water and slow down the rate at which it is lost.

The stem contains chlorophyll to take over the role of the leaves in photosynthesis.

Leaves have become spines, in order to reduce the surface area for water loss.

The stem is swollen with stored water.

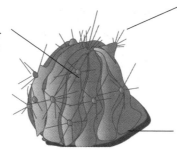

Adaptations of cactus

Fig. 1.20

Sample IGCSE questions

1.   The following diagrams show a bacterium and a virus:

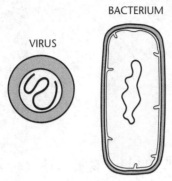

BACTERIUM

VIRUS

(a)   The real length of the bacterium is 0.002 mm.

Work out the magnification of the diagram of the bacterium.

You must show how you worked out your answer.   **[2]**

> *length of bacterial diagram = 40 mm* ✓
>
> $Magnification = \dfrac{40}{0.002} = 20000$ ✓

In this type of question make sure that you measure the cell in the same units as in the question, i.e. mm.

(b)   Apart from size, write down two differences between the structure of bacteria and viruses.   **[2]**

> *1. Bacteria contain cytoplasm but viruses do not* ✓*.*
>
> *2. Bacteria have a cell membrane but viruses do not* ✓*.*

These differences are due to the fact that viruses are not cells.

(c)   Explain why bacteria are placed in a kingdom of their own.   **[2]**

> *Bacteria do not have a nucleus, the genetic material is in the cytoplasm* ✓*.*
>
> *They are much smaller than plant or animal cells* ✓*.*

This is the main characteristic of bacteria.

(d)   Some scientists originally thought that viruses were the ancestors of all living organisms.

Explain why their method of reproduction makes that unlikely.   **[2]**

> *Viruses need living cells in order to reproduce* ✓*. If they were the ancestors of living cells they would have to be able to reproduce by themselves* ✓*.*

Sample IGCSE questions

2. The following diagram shows a bony fish.

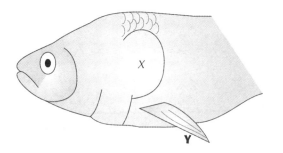

> Examiners will give you a certain margin for error but make sure you label the centre of the structure.

(a) (i) Write an X on the diagram to show the position of the gills. [1]

   (ii) What is the structure labelled Y on the diagram and what is its function? [3]

> *Structure Y is one of the paired lateral fins ✓.*
> *It is used to help the fish change direction while swimming ✓.*
> *It allows the fish to go up and down and also backwards ✓.*

(b) The following diagram shows one gill from a bony fish.

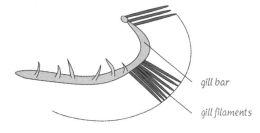

gill bar

gill filaments

(i) Complete the diagram by adding labels to the two label lines. [2]

> On a higher tier paper you will not have a choice of labels to pick from.

(ii) Write down two ways in which the gills are adapted for gaseous exchange. [2]

> *1. Gill filaments provide a large surface area ✓.*
> *2. Gill filaments have many lamellae to increase surface area ✓.*

(c) Compare the problems that fish face in moving through water with the problems that birds have in moving through air. [4]

> *The main difference is that air is less dense than water ✓.*
> *Water therefore provides more support than air and so birds need to have a strong but light skeleton ✓. Water provides more resistance to movement so fish must be very streamlined ✓. Birds must have a large surface area to push against the air ✓.*

> This is a continuous prose answer. The examiner wants you to link ideas together.

Exam practice questions

1. The diagrams A to E show five different organisms.

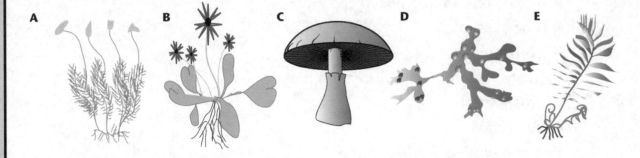

A   B   C   D   E

(a) Write down the name of the kingdom to which each of these organisms belong: **[5]**

A _____

B _____

C _____

D _____

E _____

(b) How does organism C obtain its food? **[3]**

(c) Which kingdoms are not represented by the organisms shown above? **[2]**

2. Read the following passage and answer the questions that follow:

> The Greek philosopher Aristotle was the first person to make a real attempt to classify living organisms. Aristotle only knew of several hundred living organisms and the system he devised was an artificial system.
>
> It was not until about 2000 years later that John Ray developed a natural classification system, which was then improved upon by Linnaeus.
>
> Linneaus also devised the binomial system for naming organisms that avoided much confusion.

(a) What is meant by an artificial classification system, such as the one devised by Aristotle? **[1]**

(b) (i) How does the binomial system of naming organisms work? **[2]**

     (ii) How did this naming system 'avoid much confusion'? **[3]**

(c) Aristotle was only aware that several hundred organisms existed.

Suggest reasons why Ray and Linnaeus were aware of many more organisms. **[3]**

Chapter 2

Organisation and maintenance of the organism

The following topics are covered in this section:

- Cell structure and organisation
- Levels of organisation
- Movement in and out of the cell
- Enzymes
- Nutrition in plants and animals
- Transportation in plants and animals
- Respiration
- Excretion
- Coordination and response

2.1 Cell structure and organisation

After studying this section you should be able to:

- describe the main differences between plant and animal cells
- state that the nucleus contains chromosomes
- explain how certain cells are specialised for the jobs that they do
- know that most living organisms are made of cells
- identify and describe the structure of a plant cell and an animal cell
- define tissue, organ and an organ system
- relate their structures to their functions
- calculate the magnification and size of biological specimens.

A cell can be thought of as a bag of chemicals which is capable of surviving and replicating itself. It was discovered by **Robert Hooke** in the year 1665, using a compound microscope. Inside the cell, the chemicals differ in various ways from those outside the cell. Without a barrier between the cell and the environment the chemicals would mix freely, so all living cells are surrounded by a membrane, known as the **cell membrane**.

 KEY POINT The cell is the basic unit of structure and function in living organisms.

Cross-section of a plant cell

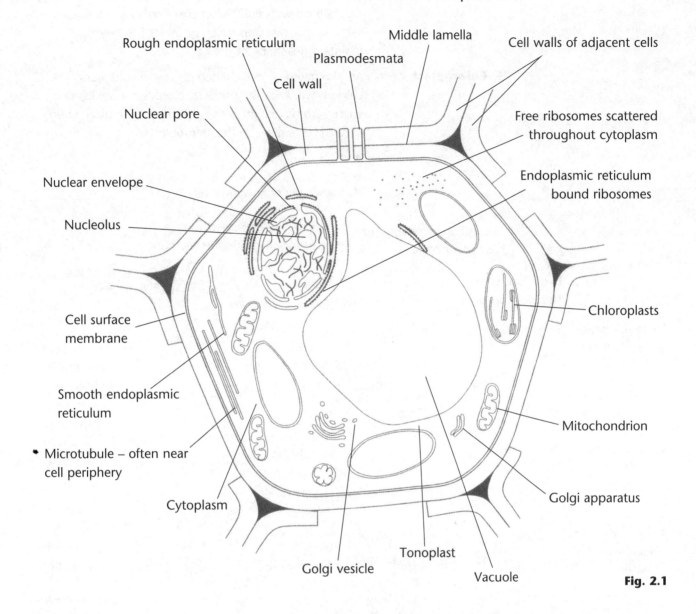

Rough endoplasmic reticulum

Middle lamella

Cell walls of adjacent cells

Plasmodesmata

Cell wall

Nuclear pore

Free ribosomes scattered throughout cytoplasm

Nuclear envelope

Endoplasmic reticulum bound ribosomes

Nucleolus

Cell surface membrane

Chloroplasts

Smooth endoplasmic reticulum

Mitochondrion

Microtubule – often near cell periphery

Cytoplasm

Golgi apparatus

Golgi vesicle

Tonoplast

Vacuole

Fig. 2.1

Structure of plant cell

1. Cell wall — A thick, rigid membrane that surrounds a plant cell. This layer of cellulose fibre provides support for the cell. The cell wall also bonds with other cell walls to form the structure of the plant.

2. Cell membrane — This thin layer of protein and fat surrounds the cell; it is semipermeable allowing some substances to pass into the cell and blocking others.

3. Nucleus — Spherical body containing many organelles, including the nucleolus. The nucleus controls many of the functions of the cell (by controlling protein synthesis) and contains DNA (in chromosomes). The nucleus is surrounded by the nuclear membrane.

4. **Vacuole** — A large, membrane-bound space within a plant cell that is filled with fluid. Most plant cells have a single vacuole that takes up much of the cell. It helps maintain the shape of the cell.

5. **Chloroplast** — An elongated or disc-shaped organelle containing chlorophyll. Photosynthesis (the process in which energy from sunlight is converted into chemical energy – food) takes place in the chloroplasts.

Cross section of an animal cell

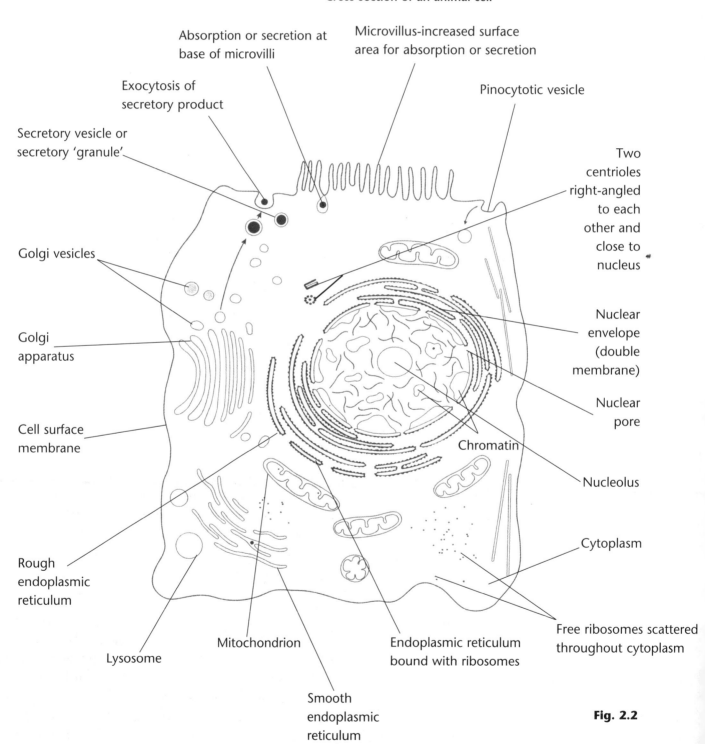

Fig. 2.2

Structure of an animal cell

1. **Cell wall**   –   Absent.

2. **Cell membrane** – A thin layer of protein and fat which surrounds the cell. The cell membrane is semi-permeable, allowing some substances to pass into the cell and blocking others.

3. **Nucleus**   –   A spherical body containing many organelles, including the nucleolus. The nucleus controls many of the functions of the cell (by controlling protein synthesis) and contains DNA (in chromosomes). The nucleus is surrounded by the nuclear membrane.

4. **Vacuole**   –   A fluid-filled, membrane-surrounded cavity inside a cell. The vacuole is filled with food being digested and waste material that is on its way out of the cell.

5. **Cytoplasm**   –   The jelly like material outside the cell nucleus in which the organelles are submerged.

Animal and plant cells

All the cell parts may not be there when matured.

Red blood cells do not have a nucleus

Xylem cells do not have a nucleus or cytoplasm.

All plant cells do not contain chloroplast. e.g., root cells

Remember that some plant cells, such as root cells, do not have chloroplasts.

Common mistake: many people think that only animals can respire. Plants also respire and so plant cells also have mitochondria.

Although plants and animals have many things in common, there are four main differences:

- plant cells have a strong cell wall made of cellulose, whereas animal cells do not

- plant cells have a large permanent vacuole containing cell sap, vacuoles in animal cells are small and temporary

- plant cells may contain chloroplasts containing chlorophyll for photosynthesis. Animal cells never contain chloroplasts

- animal cells store energy as granules of glycogen but plants store starch.

Plant and animal cells have many smaller structures in the cytoplasm. These can be seen by using an electron microscope.

 KEY POINT Mitochondria are examples of these structures and are the site of respiration in the cell.

Fig. 2.3

Nuclei, chromosomes and genes

Most cells contain a nucleus that controls all of the chemical reactions that go on in the cell. Nuclei can do this because they contain the genetic material. Genetic material controls the characteristics of an organism and is passed on from one generation to the next. The genetic material is made up of structures called chromosomes. They are made up of a chemical called **Deoxyribonucleic Acid** or **DNA**. The DNA controls the cell by coding for the making of proteins, such as enzymes. The enzymes will control all the chemical reactions taking place in the cell.

> **KEY POINT**
> A gene is a part of a chromosome that codes for one particular protein.

By controlling cells, genes therefore control all the characteristics of an organism. Different organisms have different numbers of genes and different numbers of chromosomes. In most organisms that reproduce sexually, the chromosomes can be arranged in pairs. This is because one of each pair comes from each parent.

Cell division

There seems to be a limit to how large one cell can become. If organisms are to grow, cells must split or divide. Cells also need to divide to make special sex cells called **gametes** for reproduction.

> **KEY POINT**
> Cells therefore need to divide for two main reasons – for growth or reproduction.

Because the two words meiosis and mitosis are very similar, you need to spell them correctly in order to score marks in exams.

There are two types of cell division, one for each of these two reasons:

Mitosis is used for growth → New cells ← Meiosis is used for reproduction

Fig. 2.4

Both of these two types of cell division have certain things in common. The DNA of the chromosomes has to be copied first to make new chromosomes. The chromosomes are then organised into new nuclei and the cytoplasm then divides into new cells.

In mitosis two cells are produced from one. As long as the chromosomes have been copied correctly, each new cell will have the same number of chromosomes and the same information.

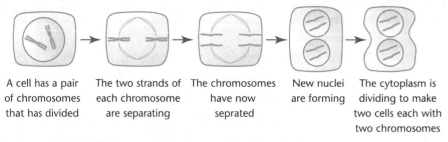

A cell has a pair of chromosomes that has divided   The two strands of each chromosome are separating   The chromosomes have now seprated   New nuclei are forming   The cytoplasm is dividing to make two cells each with two chromosomes

Fig. 2.5

In meiosis, the chromosomes are also copied once but the cell divides twice. This makes four cells each with half the number of chromosomes, one from each pair.

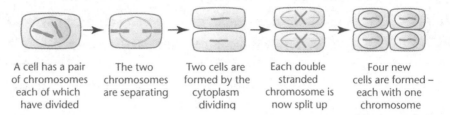

| A cell has a pair of chromosomes each of which have divided | The two chromosomes are separating | Two cells are formed by the cytoplasm dividing | Each double stranded chromosome is now split up | Four new cells are formed – each with one chromosome |

Fig. 2.6

Difference between Mitosis and Meiosis

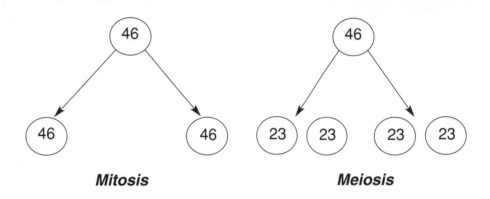

Mitosis   **Meiosis**

1. Occurs in somatic cells	1. Occurs in sex cells/genetic format
2. Full set of chromosomes are passed to daughter cell	2. Only half the chromosomes are passed to daughter cell
3. Diploid	3. Haploid
4. Chromosomes and genes in each daughter cell are identical	4. Chromosomes and genes are randomly assorted
5. Daughter cells are completely identical to the parent	5. New organisms show variation from the parent

By the process of mitosis a large number of cells can be produced. This enables organisms to grow or repair damaged tissue. The different cells contain the same gene but develop differently.

2.2 Levels of organisation

After studying this section you should be able to:

● **know what is a tissue, an organ and an organ system**

● **differentiate between different animal cells.**

Tissue – Group of cells similar in structure that work together to perform a specific function.

e.g. in a leaf there are following tissues:

upper epidermis – the top most layer which has waxy coating which protects from excessive loss of water by evaporation.

palisade cells – the chlorophyll containing cells packed closely together below the upper epidermis help to absorb maximum sunlight.

mesophyll cells – facilitate gaseous exchange by diffusion

vascular bundles – transfer water and food.

Organ – Several tissues group together to make a structure with a specific function. This is called an organ.

e.g. Stomach, lung, kidney, tongue, etc.

Organ system – A group of organs with closely related functions.

Examples are as follows:

digestive system – helps to break down complex food molecules into simple ones making it easier for assimilation

nervous system – carries messages from the organ to the brain and from the brain to different organs

muscular system ⎤ together help in movement of the
skeletal system ⎦ organism.

Animal cells become specialised to accomplish various functions. Some of these cells are summarised below.

Ciliated cells

● contain cilia which are small hair like structures

● found in respiratory tract

● carry mucous and bacteria away from the lungs.

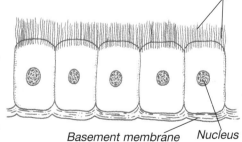

Fig. 2.7 Ciliated cells

Muscle cells

- merge together to from bundles
- these cells can contract and relax
- help in movement.

Muscle cells   **Fig. 2.8**

Red blood cells

- contain no nucleus
- contain haemoglobin
- transport oxygen to different parts of the body.

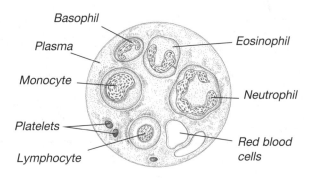

Basophil

Eosinophil

Plasma

Monocyte

Neutrophil

Platelets

Red blood cells

Lymphocyte

Blood cells   **Fig. 2.9**

Some specialised plant cells are given below.

Root hair cells

- they are extentions of the epidermis
- increase the surface area
- absorb water and mineral ions
- anchor the plant firmly to the soil.

Root hair cells   **Fig. 2.10**

Xylem cells

- long, thin cells arranged end to end to make vessels
- dead cells, so do not contain cytoplasm and nucleus
- transport water, ions from the roots to leaves
- provide mechanical support.

Xylem cells   **Fig. 2.11**

> **KEY POINT** Cells become adapted for different functions. This is called specialisation.

Specialisation allows cells to become more efficient in carrying out their jobs.

The disadvantage of being specialised is that the cells lose the ability to take over the jobs of other cells if they are lost.

An example of a specialised cell is a nerve cell or **neuron**.

Fig. 2.12

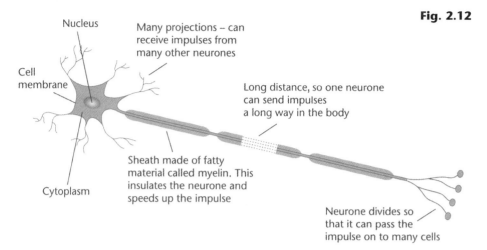

Nucleus

Many projections – can
receive impulses from
many other neurones

Cell
membrane

Long distance, so one neurone
can send impulses
a long way in the body

Sheath made of fatty
material called myelin. This
insulates the neurone and
speeds up the impulse

Cytoplasm

Neurone divides so
that it can pass the
impulse on to many cells

- cells that do similar jobs are gathered together into tissues
- more complicated organisms have organs that are made up of a number of tissues
- groups of organs work together in systems to carry out certain functions.

Cells
e.g. nerve
cells

Tissues
e.g. nerve
tissues

Organs
e.g. brain

Systems
e.g. nervous
system

Fig. 2.13

2.3 Size of specimens

LEARNING SUMMARY

After studying this section you should be able to:

● *explain how we observe a magnified image using microscope.*

$$\text{Magnification} = \frac{\text{Observed size}}{\text{Actual size}}$$

Make sure both the measurements are in the same units. There are 1000 microns in a millimeter.

The diagram of a cell is shown in the figure below, which is magnified 2.5 times. Calculate the actual size of the cell, as shown between points A and B. Show your working.

A

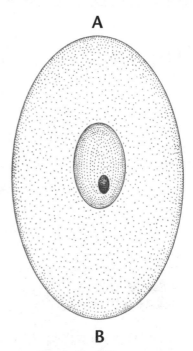

A – B = 7.5 cm

B   **Fig. 2.14**

Observed size = 7.5 cm = 75 mm

Magnification = 2.5 cm = 25 mm

Observed size = 75 mm =   3 cm/30 mm

Magnified size = 25 × 3 mm

PROGRESS CHECK

1. What are cell walls made of?
2. What is the main difference between vacuoles in plant cells and those in animal cells?
3. What do mitochondria do?
4. Place these structures in order of size, largest first:
    nucleus   mitochondrion   chloroplast   liver cell   chromosome
5. Define magnification of a cell.
6. How can you say that leaf is an organ?

6. Leaf is an organ because it is made up of tissus like the vascular bundle, epidermal and mesophyll cells that function together to make food for the plant.

5. Magnification is the number of times larger an image is compared to the real size of the object.

4. Liver cell, nucleus, chloroplast, mitochondrion, chromosome.

1. Cellulose;   2. Vacuoles in plant cells are larger and permanent;   3. Carry out respiration;

2.4 Movement in and out of cells

After studying this section you should be able to:

● understand how substances pass in and out of cells including:
  ● passively by diffusion
  ● by osmosis, which is a special type of diffusion
  ● by active transport, which requires energy
● define diffusion and osmosis
● state the importance of gaseous and solute diffusion
● give examples of diffusion and osmosis in living organisms
● describe the factors affecting both the processes.

2.4.1 Diffusion

Definition

Diffusion is the net movement of a substance from an area of high concentration to an area of low concentration. This happens down a diffusion gradient.

How does it work?

Diffusion works because particles are always moving about in a random way. This means that the particles will spread out evenly after a while.

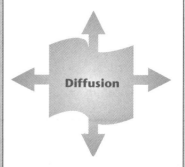

Diffusion

How fast does it work?

The rate of diffusion depends on how fast the particles move. The warmer it is, the faster they move. Smaller particles also move faster.

Examples

Oxygen diffuses into the red blood cells in the lungs and carbon dioxide diffuses out of the blood. Carbon dioxide enters and oxygen leaves leaf cells by diffusion.

Fig. 2.15: Oxygen given out of leaf

Diffusion takes place in different parts of living organisms

Site	Substance	Description
alveoli of lungs	oxygen	alveoli to blood capillaries
alveoli of lungs	carbon dioxide	blood capillaries to alveoli
stomata of leaf	oxygen	leaf to the atmosphere

Importance of diffusion in living cells

1. Absorption of oxygen into cells and the movement of carbon dioxide in the reverse direction occurs by diffusion.

2. The movement of glucose from the gut into the body cells takes place by diffusion.

3. Oxygen is transported through the air spaces to and from the cells across stomata with the help of diffusion.

Water as a solvent

1. Most of the cells are made up of about 75% water.

2. Most of the substances in the cells are transported dissolved in water.

3. Many chemical reactions take place in water.

Importance of gaseous diffusion

1. Diffusion of oxygen and carbon dioxide molecules in and out of the cells.

2. During respiration oxygen is used, reducing its concentration within the cell, which helps the cell to absorb more oxygen.

3. Carbon dioxide which is a product of respiration, increases the concentration in the cell and diffuses out.

4. Osmosis maintains the turgor pressure of the cell.

5. Translocation takes place with the help of osmosis and diffusion.

2.4.2 Osmosis

Osmosis and diffusion are called passive transports. This means that they do not need energy from the respiratory process. Their energy comes from the movement of the particles.

Osmosis is really a special kind of diffusion. It involves the movement of water molecules. It needs a:

- **Partially permeable membrane** – the cell membrane is selectively permeable because it allows certain molecules to pass through and not others. Water can pass through but dissolved substances cannot.

- **Different concentration of solution on each side of the membrane** – water will move from the weak solution (high concentration of water) to the strong solution (low concentration of water).

- **Water potential gradient** – when the number of molecules of water in the solution become less and the concentration of the solute becomes more, the water molecules move to the place where there is low concentration of water molecules.

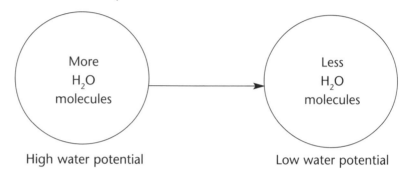

KEY POINT So water will move from high to low water potential gradient.

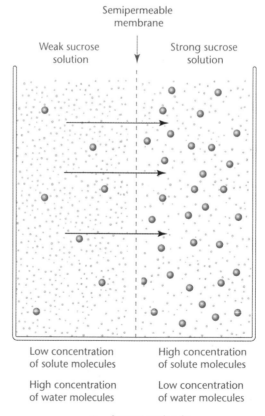

Fig. 2.16

KEY POINT

> Osmosis is the net movement of water from a dilute to a concentrated solution through a selectively permeable membrane, or we can say osmosis is the net movement of water molecules down water potential gradient from a high water potential to a low water potential.

- Plants rely on osmosis to obtain water through their roots.
- When young plants loose more water than they gain, cells become flaccid and the plant wilts.
- When we get dehydrated, the RBCs shrink and become less efficient to carry oxygen.

Importance of osmosis in animal cells

- Outside and inside the cell, concentration of liquid should be maintained to control osmosis.

 Tissue fluid ————————————➤ concentration controlled
 Blood ————————————➤ by brain and kidney

- If the cell gets more concentrated ——➤ water will move in ——➤ cell will burst
- If the cell gets less concentrated ——➤ water will move out ——➤ cell will contract and get dehydrated

Cell membranes are partially permeable, so if the solution on either side of the membrane is different osmosis will occur.

Importance of osmosis in plant cells

- Water is absorbed into the root hair by osmosis.
- Water travels from the soil to the xylem vessel with the help of osmosis.

Experiments with osmosis

When plant cells gain water by osmosis, they swell. The cell wall stops them from bursting. Osmosis can be studied by placing pieces of plant tissue into different concentrations of sugar solution. If the pieces of tissue increase in mass then water has entered the tissue by osmosis. This is because the solution is weaker than the concentration inside the cells. If the tissue loses mass then water has left the tissue. By finding the point at which there is no change in mass, the concentration inside the cells can be estimated.

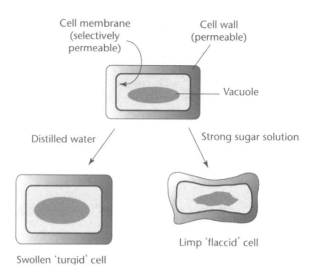

Fig. 2.17

Turgid plant cells are very important for helping to support plants. Osmosis is also important in the absorption of water by the roots.

Importance of water as a solvent

- Most cells contain about 70% of water.
- Most substances are transported dissolved in water.
- Many important reactions take place in water medium.

2.4.3 Active transport

Sometimes substances have to be moved from a place where they are in low concentration to where they are highly concentrated. This is in the opposite direction to diffusion and is called active transport.

> **Definition**
>
> Active transport is the movement of a substance against a diffusion gradient with the use of energy from respiration.

Diagram of active transport in cells.

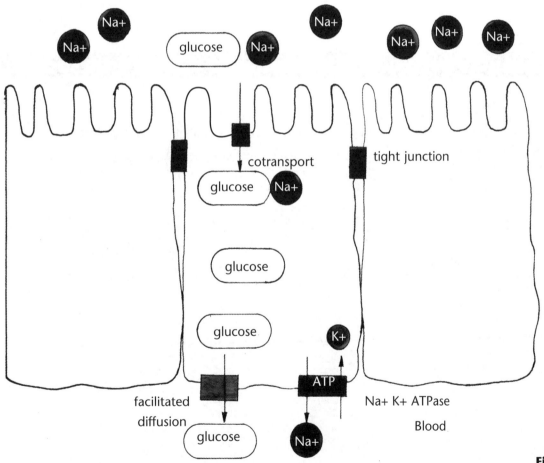

Fig. 2.18

How does it work?

Proteins in the cell membrane pick up the substance and carry it across the membrane. This requires energy, which is produced in the cell from respiration.

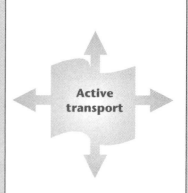

Active transport

How fast does it work?

Anything that slows down respiration will slow down the rate of active transport. This could be a poison, such as cyanide, or lack of oxygen.

Examples

Glucose is absorbed from the food into the cells of the small intestine by active transport. Minerals are absorbed into plant roots from the soil against a concentration gradient.

Fig. 2.19

Difference between diffusion and active transport

- Direction of movement (down a gradient, or up a gradient)
- Whether or not energy is needed for the movement

1. Where does the energy for diffusion come from?
2. What is a diffusion gradient?
3. Why do vegetables swell up when they are placed in a sauce-pan of water prior to cooking?
4. A person in a room is wearing strong scent. Why can people smell this scent more quickly on a warm day?
5. How is active transport different to diffusion?
6. Plant roots take up minerals very slowly from waterlogged soil. Why is this?
7. List the ways in which a cell membrane might regulate the flow of substances into the cells.
8. Give two differences between diffusion and osmosis.
9. Sometimes due to loss of water, cells become limp, weak and soft. What is this condition called?
10. Explain the terms active transport and passive transport.

1. The movement of the particles (kinetic energy); 2. This is when a substance is not spread out evenly and is in high concentration in one area and in low concentration in an adjacent area; 3. The vegetables take in water by osmosis because their cell contents are more concentrated than the water; 4. The particles have more energy and move quicker; 5. Active transport needs energy from respiration, diffusion does not. Active transport is against a diffusion gradient but diffusion is down a diffusion gradient; 6. There is less oxygen in a waterlogged soil, so respiration is slower, releasing less energy for active transport. 7. Thin membrane, turgidity, concentration gradient; 8. Diffusion – a. movement of solute particles from a region of high concentration to a region of low concentration. b. no membrane between the solutions. Osmosis – a. it is the movement of solvent particles from a region of higher concentration to a region of lower concentration 9. Wilting 10. Active transport – the movement of ions against concentration gradient with the aid of energy. Passive transport – diffusion of ions without the utilisation of energy.

2.5 Enzymes

LEARNING SUMMARY

After studying this section you should be able to:

- *define enzyme, catalyst, substrate and the end product*
- *know that enzymes are proteins*
- *explain the effect of temperature and pH on the activity of an enzyme*
- *describe the role of enzymes in germination of seeds*
- *know that the enzymes are used in food industry and washing powders.*

What are enzymes?

> **KEY POINT**
>
> Enzymes are biological catalysts. They are produced in all living organisms and control all the chemical reactions that occur.

> Remember that enzymes are present in all cells not just in the digestive system.

Most of the chemical reactions that occur in living organisms would occur too slowly without enzymes. Increased temperatures would speed up the reactions but using enzymes means that the reactions are fast enough at 37 °C.

Enzymes are protein molecules that have a particular shape. They have a slot or a groove into which the substrate fits. The reaction then takes place and the products leave the enzyme.

> The substrate in a reaction is the chemical that reacts and the product is the chemical that is made.

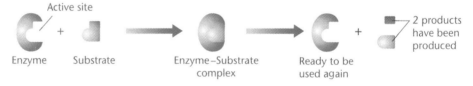

Active site

Enzyme + Substrate → Enzyme–Substrate complex → Ready to be used again + 2 products have been produced

Fig. 2.20

> **KEY POINT**
>
> This explains why enzymes are specific. Each enzyme is designed to fit only one substrate.

1. **Catalyst** — substance which increases the rate of reaction
2. **Enzyme** — a protein that acts as a biological catalyst
3. **Substrate** — the chemical compound on which the enzyme works
4. **End product** — the result of the enzymatic reaction

Most of the chemical reactions occurring in living things are helped by enzymes. Enzyme molecules are proteins which have a special shape and an active site where the substrate fits.

2.5.1 Effect of temperature on enzymes

- The optimum temperature for the enzymes to function is 37 °C which is our body temperature.
- As we increase the temperature the enzyme molecules permanently lose their shape.
- This leads to deformation of the active site and does not allow the substrate molecules to fit in. This process is called denaturation.

2.5.2 Effect of pH on enzymes

The pH of a substance is its acidity or alkalinty; some of the enzymes work in mediums other than neutral. e.g.,
- Salivary amylase – in the mouth – 6.8 pH
- Pepsin – in the stomach with hydrochloric acid – 2.0 pH
- Pancreatic lipase – in the duodenum – 9.0 pH

2.5.3 Use of enzymes in germination of seeds

The seed stores food in the form of starch in the cotyledons which is dissolved in water and converted to soluble molecules with the help of enzymes. This reaction is accelerated with the warmth provided by sunlight.

2.5.4 Biological washing powder

- Protease is added to remove stains of proteins.
- Lipase is added to remove the stains of fats and oils.
- Detergent when accompanied with enzymes makes washing more effective.
- These enzymes save energy as they work best in room temperature water.
- If boiled water is used the enzymes will get denatured.

Organisation and maintenance of the organism

2.5.5 Use of microorganisms

Use of microorganisms and fermenter to manufacture enzymes for use in biological washing powder.

● Two types of microorganisms are used – fungi and bacteria.

● They can do efficient cleaning at low temperature.

● They are mild to the fibres so can be used for larger variety of materials.

2.6 Nutrition

After studying this section you should be able to:

● *locate the parts of the digestive system and the associated organs that produce the enzymes*

● *describe the process of ingestion, digestion, absorption, assimilation and egestion*

● *identify the various types of teeth and describe their function.*

Nutrition can be defined as obtaining organic substances and mineral ions from which organisms obtain their energy and their raw materials for growth and tissue repair.

Nutritional Requirements

Plants – need carbon dioxide, water, sunlight, and chlorophyll to make their own food. The process is known as **photosynthesis**.

Animals – need seven essential nutrients: carbohydrates, proteins, fats, minerals, vitamins, water and roughage.

In a digestive system three of the main substances that need digestion, i.e. carbohydrates, proteins and fats are each broken down with the help of different types of enzymes.

There are different types of amylases, proteases and lipases produced in different parts of the gut.

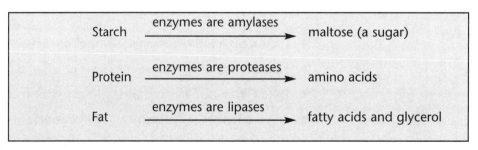

Fig. 2.21

48

Carbohydrates (C, H, O)

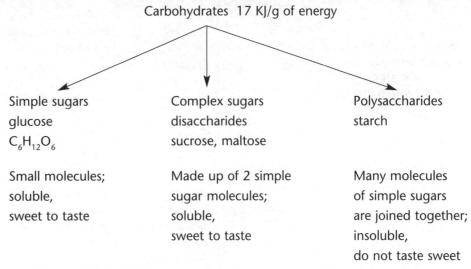

Carbohydrates 17 KJ/g of energy

Simple sugars	Complex sugars	Polysaccharides
glucose	disaccharides	starch
$C_6H_{12}O_6$	sucrose, maltose	
Small molecules; soluble, sweet to taste	Made up of 2 simple sugar molecules; soluble, sweet to taste	Many molecules of simple sugars are joined together; insoluble, do not taste sweet

Sources of carbohydrates- bread, cakes, potatoes, rice, wheat, yam.

Proteins (C, H, O, N)

- Long chains of amino acids join to form protein.
- These can join in any order forming different molecules.
- Some proteins are soluble like haemoglobin.
- Keratin (of hair, nails) is insoluble.

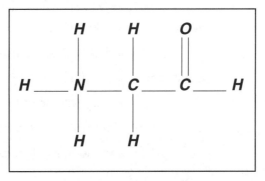

amino acid molecule

Sources of proteins – meat, fish, egg, milk, cheese, peas, beans.

Fat (C, H, O)

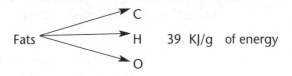

Fats → C → H   39 KJ/g of energy → O

Each fat molecule contains four molecules joined together

Glycerol + 3 fatty acids molecules ⟶ fat molecule

Sources of fats – butter, lard, margarine, oil, red meat, peanuts, cashew nuts.

In order to see if starch, proteins or fats have been digested, we can use **food tests**.

Food molecule	Substance used for test	Details of test	Sign of a positive result
starch	iodine solution	drop iodine solution into the solution to be tested	solution turns blue-black
reducing sugars	Benedict's solution	add Benedict's solution to the solution and boil in water bath for two minutes	solution turns orange-red
fats	ethanol	ethanol is shaken with the substance to be tested and then a few drops of the ethanol are dropped into water	a milky white emulsion forms in the water
protein	sodium hydroxide and copper sulphate (Biuret test)	add several drops of dilute sodium hydroxide solution followed by several drops of copper sulphate solution	solution turns purple

These tests are used to identify presence of cabohydrates, proteins or fats in a solution.

Minerals – • inorganic substances

 • needed in small amounts to prevent deficiency diseases.

 e.g. Calcium – 1. required to make bones and teeth strong
  2. found in cheese, milk, bread.

 Iron – 1. required in the haemoglobin to carry oxygen to the cells
  2. found in liver, egg yolk
  3. deficiency leads to anaemia.

Water – • helps to create a medium for metabolic reactions

 • dissolves substances for transport.

Roughage – • this fibre cannot be digested

 • roughage helps to keep the alimentary canal in good condition

 • prevents constipation

 • found in all plant cells, outer husk of cereal grain, unpolished rice.

The starch is mixed with amylase and then small amounts are tested with iodine solution to see how fast the starch is digested. If the temperatures of the water baths are measured then a graph can be plotted to show how fast the reaction occurs at different temperatures.

Vitamins – organic compounds required in small quantities for good health. They must be present in a healthy diet. If a given vitamin is lacking, a characteristic set of symptoms will develop known as deficiency disease.

 Vitamin C – found in citrus fruits (lemons, oranges) raw vegetables. It prevents scurvy.

 Vitamin D – found in butter, egg yolk or is manufactured by our own skin. It prevents rickets.

Use of microorganisms in the food industry

Yoghurt

- Bacteria are used to ferment milk at 46 °C.

- As a result lactic acid is produced which makes the milk coagulate.

- The temperature is reduced to 5 °C to stop bacterial action.

Bread

- Yeast is mixed with flour, some sugar and water to make dough.

- The dough is kept at room temperature to allow the yeast to breathe releasing CO_2.

- This CO_2 allows the dough to rise.

- When the bread is baked, the CO_2 is expelled and the yeast is killed giving a spongy bread.

Single Protein

- A protein produced by microorganisms such as bacteria, fungi or algae.

- Although it contains 72% of protein it is not good to taste.

- It is very expensive to produce.

Use of food additives

Antioxidant

- prevent oxidation which may change the colour or spoil the taste of the food.

Colourings

- improve the appearance of the food

- can trigger allergic reactions, e.g. sunset yellow.

Flavourings

- enhance the taste of food, e.g. monosodium glutamate

- can cause allergies, obesity, tooth decay, etc.

Preservatives

- give processed food a longer shelf life

- sulpher dioxide and sodium nitrate are most commonly used

- SO_2 can destroy B_1 and sodium nitrate is said to be a carcinogen.

2.6.1 Plant nutrition

After studying this section you should be able to:

- *understand photosynthesis*
- *understand the role of limiting factors*
- *understand the role of mineral salts*
- *explain the internal structure of leaf*
- *understand the importance of mineral requirements*
- *realise the dangers of overuse of nitrogenous fertilisers.*

2.6.1.1 Photosynthesis

Photosynthesis is the process by which plants make glucose, with the help of carbon dioxide and water. It uses sunlight and the green pigment chlorophyll, found in chloroplasts.

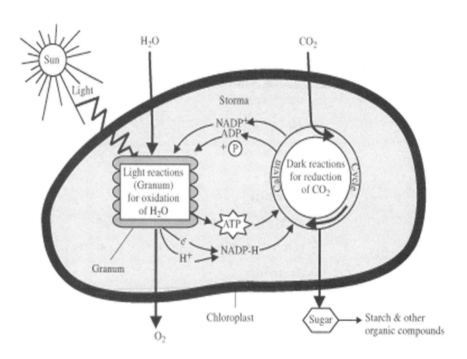

Outline of photosynthesis   **Fig. 2.22**

Process of Photosynthesis

- Green plants take in CO_2 through the stomata in the leaves by diffusion.
- Water is obtained through the root hair by osmosis from the soil and this is transported through xylem to leaves.
- Chloroplasts present in the leaf, trap light energy which is used to break up water molecules into hydrogen and oxygen ions.

- Hydrogen and CO_2 combine to form glucose.
- Glucose usually changes into sucrose for transport and is stored as starch.
- Oxygen is released as a waste product or is used for respiration.

Limiting factors

Photosynthesis is a chemical reaction. The rate or speed of this reaction is limited by the following factors:

- intensity of light
- concentration of carbon dioxide
- temperature.

KEY POINT These three factors are called limiting factors because they limit the rate of photosynthesis.

Exam questions on limiting factors usually involve graphs like these.

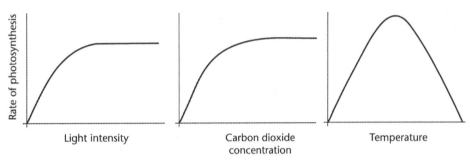

Fig. 2.23

The graphs show that as light and carbon dioxide increase, so does the rate of photosynthesis, until the rate levels out at a new optimum level. The rate is then stable until the new limiting factor is removed. **Temperature** is different – any increase above the optimum level causes the rate to slow and stop. This is because high temperature **denatures** the enzymes.

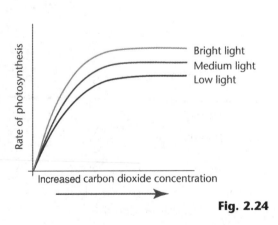

Fig. 2.24

The equation

Fig. 2.25

Remember: the equation for respiration is the equation for photosynthesis backwards.

Carbon dioxide + water $\xrightarrow[\text{Chlorophyll}]{\text{Light}}$ glucose + oxygen

The balanced equation for photosynthesis is:

$$6CO_2 + 6H_2O \rightarrow C_6H_{12}O_6 + 6O_2$$

Photosynthesis is unique to green plants and it is the final light energy trapping process on which all life ultimately depends.

This is the only biological process which releases oxygen into the atmosphere.

> **KEY POINT**   Oxygen supports life on earth.

2.6.1.2 Leaf Structure

Cross section of leaf

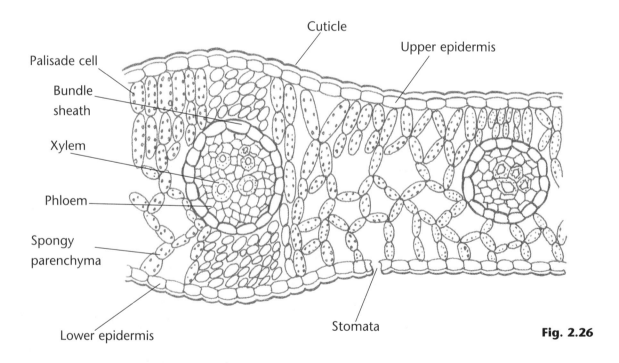

Cuticle
Upper epidermis
Palisade cell
Bundle sheath
Xylem
Phloem
Spongy parenchyma
Lower epidermis
Stomata

Fig. 2.26

Mango (*Mangifera indica*): Transverse section of leaf

Functions of a leaf

1. Broad, wide and flat leaf blade provides large area for absorption of light and carbon dioxide.

2. Spongy parenchyma helps in easy diffusion.

3. Palisade cells with large number of chloroplasts are suitable for absorption of maximum light.

4. Network of veins enables the supply of water and minerals and translocation of food.

5. Placement of stomata and guard cells helps to regulate the flow of substances in and out of the leaf.

Chloroplasts are mainly found near the upper surface of the leaf. They absorb energy from sunlight in order to power the reaction.

Stomata are found on the under surface of the leaf. They open during the day to absorb carbon dioxide and release oxygen. They close at night in order to stop the loss of water.

The **vascular bundles** contain **xylem** vessels, which transport water and **phloem** vessels, which transport glucose.

You must remember that respiration continues all the time.

Photosynthesis versus respiration

KEY POINT Photosynthesis only occurs during the hours of daylight. Plants respire all the time.

A common error is that many students think that plants only respire at night.

However, during the day, photosynthesis proceeds much faster than respiration, so it is easy to see why some students make this mistake.

There are two times during the day when photosynthesis and respiration are equal. At these times, the carbon dioxide being used by photosynthesis is equal to the carbon dioxide being produced by respiration.

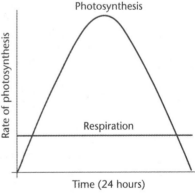

Fig. 2.27

Carbon dioxide enrichment in green house systems

Only 0.04% of the atmospheric air is carbon dioxide, so it is one of the limiting factors of photosynthesis. Since a green house is a closed system the content of air can be controlled. The amount of carbon dioxide can be increased either by burning fossil fuels or by releasing pure carbon dioxide into the system.

Optimum light

Light is another limiting factor of photosynthesis, but this can be enhanced by providing artificial light, specially during winter.

Optimum temperature

If temperature falls during winter, it can be warmed up either by burning fossil fuels (where it is beneficial in increasing the amount of carbon dioxide also) or by heating systems.

What next?

Once glucose has been made in the chloroplasts, many different things can happen to it.

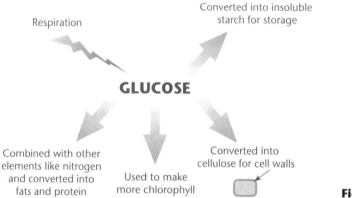

Fig. 2.28

2.6.1.3 Mineral requirements

Mineral requirements for plants

Nitrate ions

- Nitrate ions are very important for the syntheses of protein and nucleic acid.

- Nitrates are used particularly where growth occurs and enzymes are synthesised.

Nitrogen deficiency leads to the following:

- reduced protein synthesis and reduced growth of all organs

- weakness of stem

- lower leaves become yellow and fall, while upper leaves turn pale.

Magnesium ions

Magnesium plays a very active role in chlorophyll synthesis.

Magnesium deficiency leads to the following:

- plants will not be able to make chlorophyll

- leaves turn yellow from the bottom of the stem

- reduced chlorophyll will reduce photosynthesis

- yellowing of leaves due to deficiency of Magnesium ions is called chlorosis.

Mineral salts

For healthy growth, plants also need mineral salts:

- **nitrates** to make proteins

- **magnesium** to make chlorophyll.

A lack of these minerals has serious effects on plants.

Fig. 2.29

| **no nitrates** | **no phosphates** | **no potassium** | **no magnesium** |
| stunted growth yellow older leaves | purple younger leaves | yellow leaves with dead spots | stunted growth pale yellow leaves |

PROGRESS CHECK

1. Write out a balanced equation for photosynthesis.
2. How many molecules of glucose are made from six molecules of water and six molecules of carbon dioxide?
3. Explain how a leaf is adapted to its function.
4. On a normal sunny day, how many times does the rate of photosynthesis equal the rate of respiration?
5. List three limiting factors for photosynthesis and explain which is the odd one out.
6. State five things that can happen to glucose after it is made during photosynthesis.
7. Name four mineral salts needed by plants and for each one explain how the plant uses it and what happens when it is missing.
8. What are autotrophs?
9. Where do the green plants get their raw materials for photosynthesis?
10. What happens to the oxygen produced as a by-product during photosynthesis?
11. What is the function of palisade cells ?
12. What do the network veins help in?
13. When can we expect the stomata to be closed?

13. When there is either excess or shortage of water in the environment.
12. Conducting water with minerals and food made in the leaves to other parts of the leaf.
11. To trap sunlight.
10. Given out of the plant through the stomata in the leaves.
9. Carbon dioxide from the air, warmth from the sunlight, water and minerals from the soil.
8. Organisms which can make their own food from inorganic substances.
Stunted yellow leaves.
Potassium to help enzymes. Yellow leaves with dead spots. Magnesium to make chlorophyll.
leaves. Phosphates for chemical reactions. Stunted growth and purple younger leaves.
more chlorophyll or for respiration;   7. Nitrates for proteins. Stunted growth and yellow older
its too high, enzymes get denatured;   6. Converted to starch, protein, cellulose. Used to make
4. Two;   5. Light, carbon dioxide and temperature. Temperature is the odd one out because if
vascular bundles for transport and stomata to absorb carbon dioxide and release oxygen;
1. $6CO_2 + 6H_2O \rightarrow C_6H_{12}O_6 + 6O_2$;   2. One;   3. Thin, light, large surface area, has

2.6.2 Animal nutrition

After studying this section you should be able to:

LEARNING
SUMMARY

- identify the components of a balanced diet and explain their roles
- explain how certain diseases are caused by the lack of a balanced diet
- realise that dietary requirements vary in different people
- understand how the teeth and digestive systems of animals are adapted to different diets
- understand the main causes of diseases
- describe how the body protects itself against disease.

2.6.2.1 Diet

Food and feeding

A balanced diet

The body needs the correct combination of seven different types of food substances in the diet in order to remain healthy. These substances must be combined in the correct amounts.

> **Remember: a balanced diet is not 'enough' of each type of substance but the correct amount.**

> **KEY POINT**
> The intake of the correct amounts of these food substances is called a balanced diet.

Different food substances are needed in the body for different functions and are obtained from different foods. A mixture of different foods is therefore needed in a balanced diet. The functions of many of these food substances have been discovered by observing the changes that occur in a body due to the deficiency of each particular substance.

> **KEY POINT**
> A disease caused by the lack of a food substance is called a deficiency disease.

Food substance	Use in the body	Deficiency disease	Good food source
Protein	growth and repair of cells, making enzymes	kwashiorkor: swollen abdomen, loss of hair	meat, fish, soyabean
Digestible carbohydrate	supply of energy (glycogen is a store of energy, sugars are a ready supply)	lack of carbohydrate is often linked to lack of enough food of any type, i.e. starvation	rice, potatoes, cereals
Fats	store of energy	lack of certain fatty acids may cause various diseases	dairy produce, meat, fish, nuts
Vitamins A C D	to make light sensitive chemical to make connective tissue to absorb enough calcium from the intestine	poor night vision scurvy: poor healing of wounds and bleeding gums rickets: weak bones	cod liver oil, butter citrus fruit, fresh vegetables dairy produce (can be made by sunlight on the skin)
Minerals iron calcium	to produce haemoglobin for red blood cells strengthening bones and teeth	anaemia: lack of red blood cells rickets and poorly developed teeth	liver, egg yolk dairy produce, bread
Fibre	to allow the correct rate of peristalsis	constipation, appendicitis and bowel cancer	wholemeal bread, fruit

In western society it is common to find diseases that are caused by excess intake of a substance than deficiency diseases. Examples are:

Too much fat (particularly animal fat) can cause blockages of the coronary arteries of the heart leading to **coronary heart disease**.	Too much sugar in the diet may lead to acid production by bacteria in the mouth leading to **tooth decay**.	Too much salt in the diet may lead to increased blood volume and so increased **blood pressure**.

Dietary requirements

The quantity of these seven different food substances required to make a balanced diet depends on a number of factors. These include:

> **Girls often undergo an adolescent growth spurt before boys.**

- *age* – babies have large requirements for most substances compared to their size because they are growing. This growth slows down but then adolescents will need large amounts of proteins and other nutrients as they undergo a growth spurt

- *sex* – women need more iron to replace blood lost in menstruation. These requirements change due to the difference in hormonal behaviour.

- *level of physical activity* – people with high levels of physical activity will need large amounts of energy rich foods in their diet

> **Breast feeding will also increase demands.**

- *pregnancy* – pregnant women need extra nutrients to supply the baby with its requirements for growth.

Drugs and alcohol

Drug	:	a substance which changes the way the body works.
Alcohol	:	the most widely used depressant in the world.

Effects of Alcoholism	cirrhosis
	brain damage
	dehydration

Effects on social life	reflexes become slow
	financial problems
	family ties are disturbed
	may become aggressive
	may lead to accidents

Malnutrition

This is the result of not eating a balanced diet. This may happen by consuming either too much food or too little of it. Therefore malnutrition is not only a result of poverty but is also caused by unhealthy eating habits. The diet could be lacking in one or more of the key nutrients.

Effects

- Too much food, carbohydrate and fats lead to obesity – this is the main cause of coronary heart disease and diabetes.

- Excess animal fat results in high cholesterol levels – this blocks the coronary arteries resulting in coronary heart disease.

- Too little food can lead to starvation. Excessive slimming diets can result in anorexia nervosa.

- Lack of fibre in the diet leads to constipation.

- All diseases that are caused due to the deficiency of vitamins and minerals are the result of malnutrition.

World food supplies and causes of famine

- Due to population growth there is not always enough food.
- A severe food shortage can lead to famine.
- There are two types of foods produced – perishable and non-perishable.
- Perishable foods have to be preserved by chilling, using auxins, etc.

Causes of famine

- Climate change and natural disaster
- Poverty
- Urbanisation
- Pest damage or diseases
- Poor education of farmers and old farming practices and tools

2.6.2.2 Human alimentary canal

Steps of nutrition

Ingestion	Consuming complex food (also called feeding)
Digestion	Breaking down of complex food components into simple soluble substances which can be assimilated
Absorption	Passing of simple sugars, amino acids, fatty acids and glycerol through the intestinal wall into the blood
Assimilation	Utilisation of digested food by different body cells, so that it becomes part of cell protoplasm and provides energy and material for growth and repair
Egestion	Elimination of undigested food residue as faeces

Alimentary canal and its parts

1. **Buccal cavity**
   a. two sets of teeth, milk teeth and a permanent set; there are four types of teeth that help in mastication
   b. tongue tastes the food; enables the movement of food in the buccal cavity
   c. salivary glands are in three pairs; they moisten and lubricate the food, making it easier for swallowing; salivary amylase enzyme converts starch into maltose.

2. **Pharynx**
   a. buccal cavity opens into the pharynx which contains nasal, tracheal and oesophageal openings
   b. epiglottis prevents food from entering into trachea.

3. **Oesophagus**
   a. a muscular tube which is 10 inches long
   b. peristaltic movement pushes the food down.

4. **Stomach**
   a. muscular bag which churns the food and forms chyme
   b. gastric juices contain HCl, pepsin and mucus
   c HCl kills bacteria present in food and creates an acidic medium
   d. pepsin works only in acidic medium and breaks down proteins.

5. **Small intestine** – about 6 m /20 ft long. It consists of three parts – duodenum, jejunum and ileum.

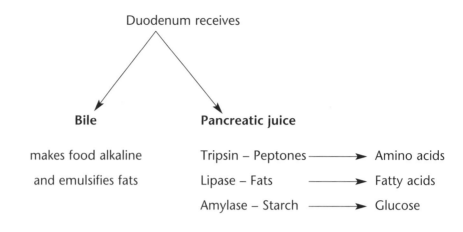

Duodenum receives

Bile

Pancreatic juice

makes food alkaline
and emulsifies fats

Tripsin – Peptones ⟶ Amino acids

Lipase – Fats ⟶ Fatty acids

Amylase – Starch ⟶ Glucose

Human alimentary canal

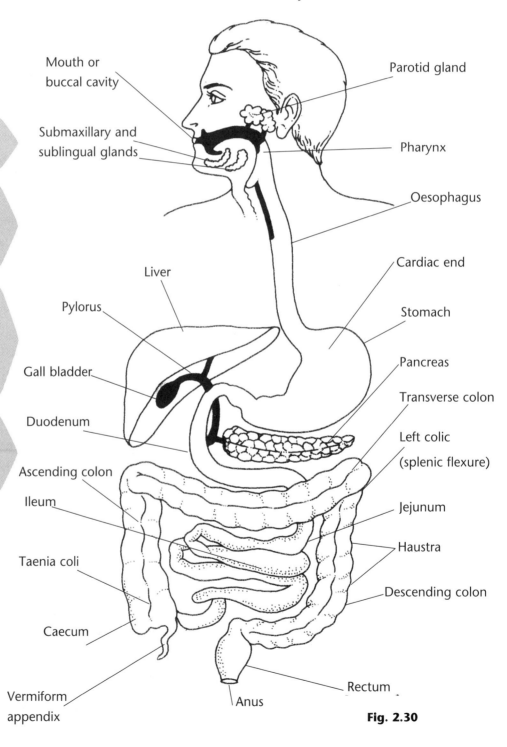

Saliva also contains
mucus to lubricate
the food.

Food is moved
down the digestive
system by muscular
contractions called
peristalsis.

Bile salts are not
enzymes. They make
the surface area of
the fat droplets
larger so lipase
works faster. This is
called emulsification.

Secretions from the
pancreas and liver are
alkaline. These help to
neutralise the acid
from the stomach.

Mouth or
buccal cavity

Submaxillary and
sublingual glands

Liver

Pylorus

Gall bladder

Duodenum

Ascending colon

Ileum

Taenia coli

Caecum

Vermiform
appendix

Parotid gland

Pharynx

Oesophagus

Cardiac end

Stomach

Pancreas

Transverse colon

Left colic
(splenic flexure)

Jejunum

Haustra

Descending colon

Rectum

Anus

Fig. 2.30

The third part of the small intestine is called the **ileum**. This is where **absorption** takes place. The ileum is specially adapted so that absorption can be speeded up. The surface area is increased because:

- the ileum is very long – about 5 metres in man
- the inside of the ileum is folded
- the folds have thousands of finger-like projections called **villi**
- the cells on the villi have projections called **microvilli**.

In order for the body to use food substances, they must get into the blood stream.

These adaptations increase the surface area by up to 600 times.

The **villi** contain large numbers of capillaries to absorb the products of digestion. Other vessels called **lacteals** mainly absorb the products of fat digestion.

Lacteals empty their contents into the bloodstream near the heart.

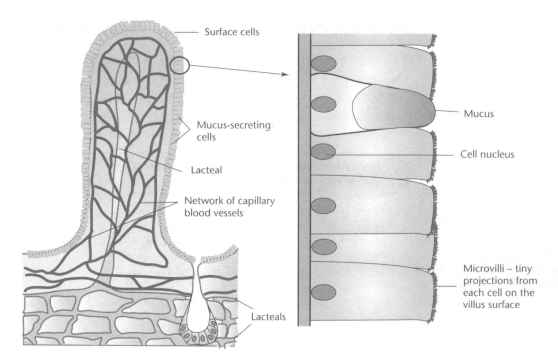

Surface cells

Mucus-secreting cells

Lacteal

Network of capillary blood vessels

Lacteals

Mucus

Cell nucleus

Microvilli – tiny projections from each cell on the villus surface

Fig. 2.31

Small intestine functions

a. serves for both digestion and absorption of digested food

b. villi increase the surface area for absorption.

6. **Large intestine**
   a. about 1.5–1.8 m in length
   b. divided into caecum, colon and rectum
   c. rectum absorbs excess water from the undigested food
   d. secretes mucus
   e. stores faeces till egestion.

7. **Anus**
   a. opening of the alimentary canal for egestion
   b. anus has circular muscle to keep it closed.

Functions of liver

- converts glucose into glycogen
- removes excess amino acids (deamination) by converting into urea which is less toxic
- destroys dead and worn out red blood cells
- produces enzymes which help in blood clotting
- synthesises vitamin A and stores other vitamins too.

> **KEY POINT**
> Simple sugars, amino acids, fatty acids and glycerol are all small enough to pass through the lining of the intestine into the blood stream. This is called absorption.

Different types of feeding in mammals

Mammals have teeth which are used to bite food and chew it. Teeth have different shapes and this makes them suited to a particular function. The selection of teeth that an animal possesses depends on the type of food that it eats.

> **KEY POINT**
> Humans have four types of teeth. This allows them to eat a range of plant and animal material.

Remember: breaking food down into smaller pieces gives enzymes a larger surface area to attack.

Premolars may have one or two roots, molars have two or three.

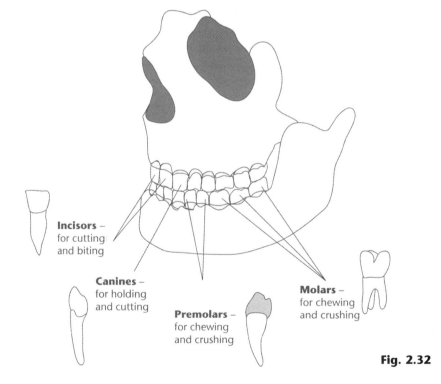

Incisors – for cutting and biting

Canines – for holding and cutting

Premolars – for chewing and crushing

Molars – for chewing and crushing

Fig. 2.32

Causes of dental decay

- The mouth has a natural microflora of bacteria which can be pathogenic.

- Plaque is the deposit formed on the surface and between the teeth from a mixture of food debris, saliva and bacteria.

- This plaque contains bacteria which acts on sugar to produce acids which corrode the enamel of the tooth.

- Then it passes to the dentine which is softer and so dissolves faster.

- It then reaches the pulp cavity and then the nerve, feeding the tooth.

- Due to this progressive activity the tooth may loosen or cause pain.

Proper care of teeth

- Avoid sugary foods and wash mouth out after every meal.

- Regular and careful brushing of teeth to prevent plaque build up.

- Use fluoride tooth paste – it hardens the enamel of the tooth.

- Monthly dental check ups to detect any tooth decay and prevent any plaque formation.

Importance of fluoride

- An appropriate intake of fluoride decreases the incidence of dental caries as it has the ability to harden the enamel of the tooth. It can be taken either dissolved in water or in a tooth paste.

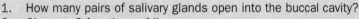

PROGRESS CHECK

1. How many pairs of salivary glands open into the buccal cavity?
2. Give any 2 functions of liver.
3. How does the small intestine adapt itself for efficient absorption of digested food?
4. Name the medium (alkaline/acidic) of the following juices.
   a. Saliva b. Gastric juice c. Bile juice d. Intestinal juice
5. List the various steps of holozoic nutrition.

1. Three pairs; 2. Converts excess blood sugar into glycogen, removes excess amino acids; 3. The small intestine has villi that increase the surface area for absorption of digested food; 4. Saliva – alkaline, Gastric juice – acidic, Bile – alkaline, Intestinal juice – alkaline; 5. Ingestion, digestion, absorption, assimilation, egestion.

2.7 Transport in plants

LEARNING SUMMARY

After learning this section you should be able to:

- *know how water uptake takes place*
- *define transpiration*
- *explain the factors affecting transpiration*
- *understand wilting*
- *know what is translocation.*

Water uptake

- Through the process of osmosis, water and minerals are absorbed by the root hair cells from the soil.

- Water passes from the cells of the root to reach the xylem vessel, from there it travels up to the stem, into the leaves.

- Water moves from the soil into the root hair along the water potential gradient as it is higher in the soil than the cell.

- There is a difference in water potential in each cell to balance it, water moves by osmosis into the next cell.

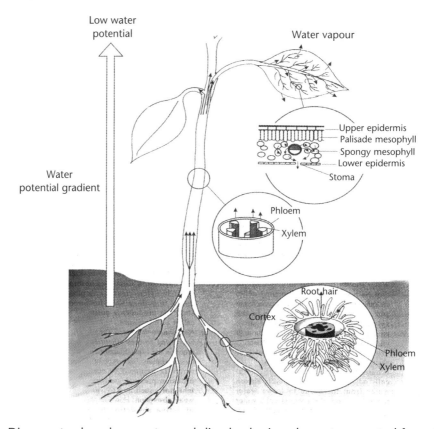

Diagram to show how water and dissolved minerals are transported from the soil up to the leaf of a plant.

Fig. 2.33

Uptake of water and minerals is carried out with the help of xylem tissue which is an essential part of vascular bundle. Xylem consists of four parts, tracheid, vessel, xylem fibre and parenchyma which together transport the sap (i.e. minerals dissolved in water) to the leaves where plant food is prepared by the process of photosynthesis.

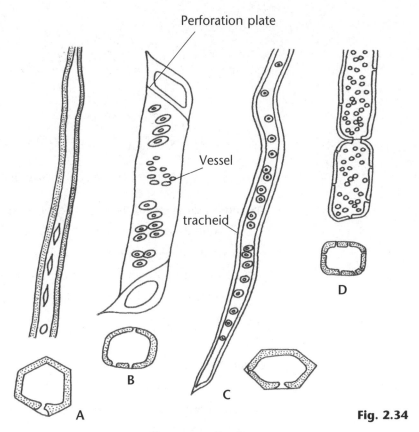

Perforation plate

Vessel

tracheid

D

B

C

A

Fig. 2.34

Elements of xylem:

A. Tracheids, B. Vessel, C. Fibre, D. Parenchyma

Transpiration – Loss of water vapour from the leaves through the stomata by the process of diffusion is called transpiration.

This physiological process creates a transpiration pull which helps in more uptake of water as well as more transport of raw materials of plant food, i.e. water and minerals.

 KEY POINT Stomata are the small pores on the leaf surface that leave the excess water by the process of diffusion.

Transpiration depends on:

A. **Light intensity** – when there is more light the stomata open up for gas exchange and water vapour diffuses out

B. **Surface area** – if surface area is greater, so is the number of stomata and the loss of water increases

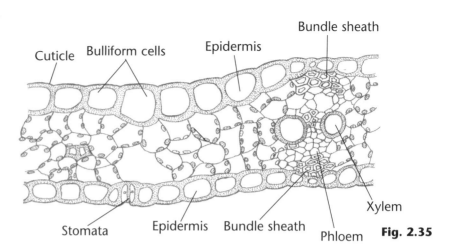

Maize (*Zea mays*): Transverse section of leaf

Wilting – Wilting means the loss of rigidity of non-woody parts of plants. It diminishes the plant's ability to transpire and grow.

It mostly occurs during afternoon hours when the roots are not able to absorb an adequate amount of water from the soil in order to compensate for the rapid loss of water from the exposed parts.

The force of cohesion is more than the force of adhesion. So the molecules are pulled up.

Water does not travel by osmosis through xylem vessels because osmosis occurs through the cell membrane.

Translocation – Food is manufactured by the green cells of leaves. Stem and root obtain their food supply from the leaves. This movement of food in aqueous solution takes place through the **phloem tissue** and is called translocation.

Phloem, the tissue of translocation consists of sieve tube, companion cell, phloem parenchyma and phloem fibre.

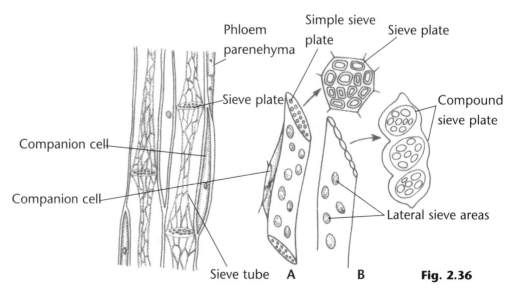

Elements of Phloem

1. Name the principal water conducting tissue in plants.
2. How do you account for the ascent of sap in plants to great heights?
3. Differentiate between transpiration and translocation.
4. What is the importance of transpiration in plants?
5. Write short notes on the following:
   a. stomatal transpiration
   b. translocation of solutes
   c. ascent of sap
   d. osmosis.
6. Name the tissue which transports food in plants.
7. What do you mean by translocation with respect to transport in plants?
8. Name the conducting tissue in plants which is living.

PROGRESS CHECK

1. Xylem.
2. According to the cohesion theory, water with the help of force of cohesion and the transpirational pull, caused by evaporation, is pulled up in the xylem vessels.
3. The loss of water in the form of vapour from the aerial parts of the plant is known as transpiration.
   The movement of food materials from the green cells of the leaves or from their storage organs in plants is called translocation.
4. Helps in absorption of water and minerals from the soil, develops a suction force which helps in the ascent of sap, translocation of water and minerals throughout the plant, provides a cooling effect, maintains the concentration of sap.
5. a. stomatal transpiration – stomata have guard cells which control the opening and closing of the stomata. 80–90% of water is lost through stomata.
   b. translocation of solutes – the food that is stored and manufactured are in insoluble form this food is converted to soluble form and then transported to different parts of the plant.
   c. ascent of sap – upward movement of water and mineral salts in the lumen of xylem vessels through the stem to its leaves, flowers and other parts of plant.
   d. osmosis – Passage of solvent molecules from a solution of its higher concentration to a solution of its lower concentration through a semi-permeable membrane.
6. Phloem cells.
7. Transport of food from the leaves to other parts of the plant.
8. Phloem.

2.8 Transport in humans

After studying this section you should be able to:

- describe the structure and functions of blood
- describe the blood vessels that carry blood around the body
- explain how the heart circulates blood and how substances are exchanged at the tissues
- describe the structure and the function of the heart
- understand double circulation and its importance
- describe the blood vessls that carry blood around the body
- know the components of blood
- discuss the process and importance of clotting
- understand the causes of heart attack and how to prevent it
- explain the components and functions of the lymphatic system
- describe the immune system, its components and its importance

2.8.1 Blood

KEY POINT Blood consists of a straw-coloured liquid called plasma in which are suspended white blood cells, red blood cells and platelets.

The plasma and cells in blood can be separated by spinning blood in a machine called a centrifuge.

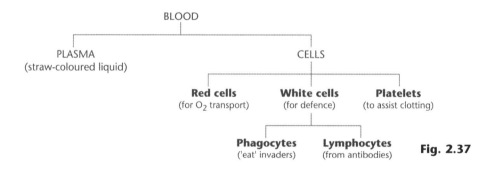

BLOOD

PLASMA
(straw-coloured liquid)

CELLS

Red cells
(for O$_2$ transport)

White cells
(for defence)

Platelets
(to assist clotting)

Phagocytes
('eat' invaders)

Lymphocytes
(from antibodies)

Fig. 2.37

The **plasma** is about 90% water but it has a number of other chemicals dissolved in it:

- blood proteins, including some that work together with the platelets to make the blood clot
- food substances, such as glucose and amino acids
- hormones
- waste materials, such as urea
- mineral salts, such as hydrogen carbonate, the main method of carrying CO$_2$.

KEY POINT Red blood cells are biconcave discs with no nucleus. They contain haemoglobin which carries oxygen around the body.

The structure of red blood cells makes them adapted for their job of picking up and carrying oxygen

The arteries and veins that pass the blood to the lungs and back are respectively known as pulmonary artery and pulmonary vein.

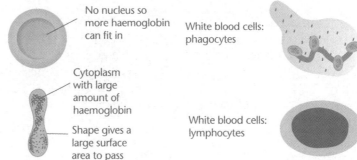

No nucleus so more haemoglobin can fit in

Cytoplasm with large amount of haemoglobin

Shape gives a large surface area to pass oxygen through

White blood cells: phagocytes

White blood cells: lymphocytes

Fig. 2.38

KEY POINT

There are two main types of white blood cell:
- phagocytes engulf foreign cells, such as bacteria
- lymphocytes make proteins called antibodies that kill invading cells.

Identification of blood cells

White Blood Cells

- lobed nucleus
- can show amoeboid movement
- can move out of the blood vessels by amoeboid movement
- short life span

Red blood cells

- discoidal biconcave shape
- no nucleus at maturity
- heamoglobin is present
- the life span is 120 days
- these are produced in the bone marrow

Platelets

- formed in the bone marrow
- these are irregular in shape
- no nucleus is present
- these help in blood coagulation

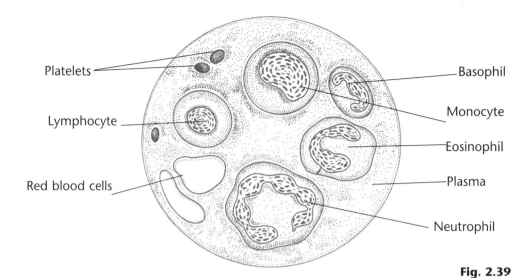

Platelets

Lymphocyte

Red blood cells

Basophil

Monocyte

Eosinophil

Plasma

Neutrophil

Fig. 2.39

Blood cells

2.8.2 Blood vessels

Until the 17th century, scientists had little idea how blood flowed around the body. In 1628 **Sir William Harvey** published the results of his studies on the circulation of blood. He was the first person to work out the jobs of the three different types of blood vessels.

> **KEY POINT** Arteries always carry blood away from the heart and veins carry blood back to the heart. Capillaries join the arteries to the veins.

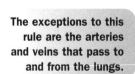
Harvey could not see capillaries but predicted that they must exist.

The three types of blood vessel are quite different in terms of their structure because they are adapted to do different jobs:

Remember: arteries = A for away from the heart.

Arteries	Capillaries	Veins
The blood is carried away from the heart and so the pressure is high	The pressure is lower than in arteries but is still high enough to make the plasma squeeze out into the tissues	The blood returning to the heart is under low pressure
Thick wall with plenty of elastic and muscle tissue	Wall is one cell thick so that plasma can leak out	Wall is thinner than in arteries

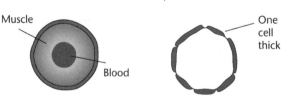

Muscle

Blood

One cell thick

Blood

Muscle

The exceptions to this rule are the arteries and veins that pass to and from the lungs.

Blood is usually oxygenated	The site of oxygen exchange with the tissues	Blood is usually deoxygenated
Valves are not needed	No valves	Valves are present to stop back-flow of blood as the pressure is low

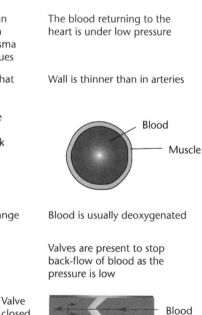

Valve closed

Blood flow

Fig. 2.40 Lumen is narrow; wall is non-collapsible. It contains more O_2

Lumen is wide; wall is collapsible. It contains more CO_2

Exchange at the tissues

When the blood flows through the capillaries, the thin walls of the capillaries allow different substances to leave or enter the blood. The direction of movement of these substances is different in different parts of the body:

● capillaries in the lungs

In the lungs CO_2 diffuses out of blood and into the air sacs and O_2 diffuses into the blood.

> Tissue fluid does not form in the lungs. If it did it would stop gaseous exchange.

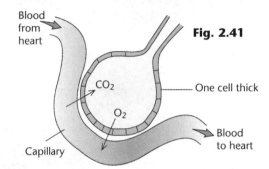

Blood from heart

Fig. 2.41

CO_2

One cell thick

O_2

Capillary

Blood to heart

● capillaries in the other tissues of the body.

The high pressure of the blood causes some of the plasma to be squeezed out of the capillaries. This is called **tissue fluid** and it carries glucose, amino acids and other useful substances to the cells.

In the rest of the tissues of the body, CO_2 diffuses into the capillaries and O_2 diffuses out of the blood into the tissues.

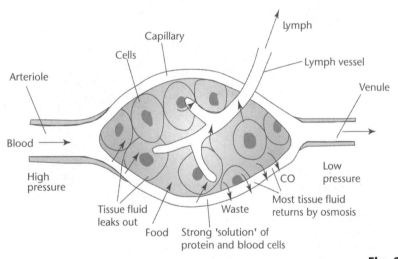

lymph

Capillary

Cells

Lymph vessel

Arteriole

Venule

Blood →

High pressure

Low pressure

CO

Tissue fluid leaks out

Waste

Most tissue fluid returns by osmosis

Food

Strong 'solution' of protein and blood cells

Fig. 2.42

The circulation

The blood is circulated around the body by the **heart**. The heart is a muscular pump made of a special type of tissue called cardiac muscle.

>
> **KEY POINT**
> The circulation in mammals is called a double circulation. This is because the blood is sent from the heart to the lungs to be oxygenated, but then returns to the heart to be pumped to the body.

The big advantage of a double circulation is that the blood is returned to the heart to gain high enough pressure to get through the capillaries of the body.

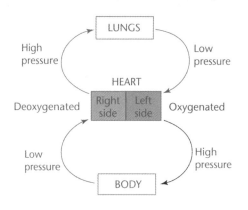

Fig. 2.43

Having a **double circulation** means that the heart has to deal with both deoxygenated and oxygenated blood at the same time. This means that the blood in the left and right side of the heart must not mix.

KEY POINT The right side of the heart carries deoxygenated blood that has returned from the body and is pumped to the lungs. The left side of the heart carries oxygenated blood.

2.8.3 Heart

This is an important diagram to learn. Remember that the right side of the heart is on the left as you look at it.

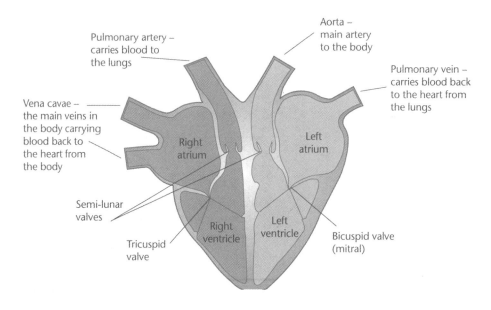

Notice that the wall of the left ventricle is thicker than the right ventricle. This is because it has to pump the blood further.

Fig. 2.44

Structure of the Heart

- It is a muscular organ – made up of the cardiac muscles.
- It is placed in the chest cavity
- It is covered by the pericardium – which is double layered and is filled with pericardial fluid.
- Pericardial fluid helps to absorb the shock – so is protective in nature.

Function of the heart

- Heart acts like a pump.
- The blood is pumped from the atria to the ventricles.
- The blood follows the following route:

As shown both the atria contract together. Thus blood from both sides reaches the ventricles simultaneously. From the ventricles the blood is pumped in the respective arteries together. Similarly, the blood from the lungs and the body reaches the atria simultaneously.

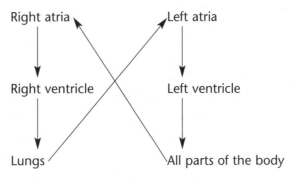

This is called a **double circulatory system**

Exercise

↓

More energy is required

↓

More oxygen required by the muscles

↓

Heart rate means the number of times the heart beats in one minute.

Blood should come to the vessels rapidly

↓

Heart pumps the blood more rapidly

↓

Heart rate increases

↓

Heart beats faster

PROGRESS CHECK

1. What substances are dissolved in plasma?
2. Why are red blood cells shaped like a biconcave disc?
3. What is the definition of an artery?
4. Why are the walls of capillaries only one cell thick?
5. What is the function of the valves in the heart?
6. What is tissue fluid?

1. Proteins, dissolved food substances, minerals, waste substances, hormones; 2. To provide a larger surface area so that they can exchange oxygen faster; 3. A blood vessel that carries blood away from the heart; 4. This allows gases to diffuse across and some of the plasma to be squeezed out; 5. They stop the blood flowing backwards, i.e. back into the atria from the ventricles or back into the ventricles from the arteries; 6. This is the part of plasma that is squeezed out of the capillaries at the tissues in order to supply the cells with useful substances.

Functions of Blood

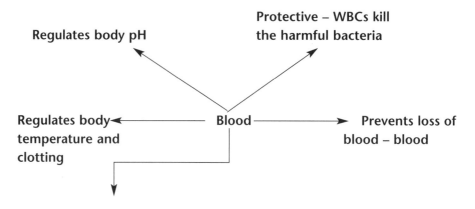

Regulates body pH

Protective – WBCs kill the harmful bacteria

Regulates body temperature and clotting ← Blood → Prevents loss of blood – blood

Transporting:
- oxygen from lungs to all parts of the body
- carbon dioxide from the cells to the lungs
- digested food from the small intestine to all parts of the body
- nitrogenous waste from the cells to the kidneys
- hormones from the site of production to the site of action.

Blood clotting (Coagulation)

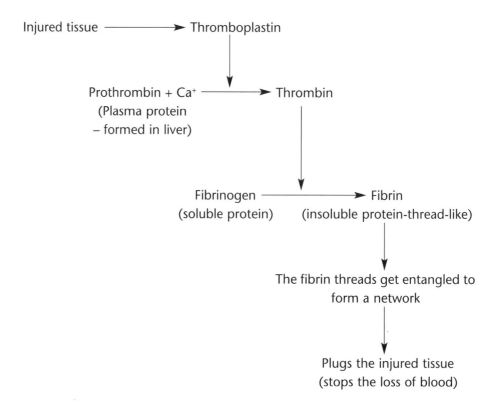

Injured tissue → Thromboplastin

Prothrombin + Ca⁺
(Plasma protein
– formed in liver) → Thrombin

Fibrinogen → Fibrin
(soluble protein) (insoluble protein-thread-like)

The fibrin threads get entangled to form a network

Plugs the injured tissue
(stops the loss of blood)

Heart attack

A heart-attack occurs when someone develops a blockage in one of the arteries (coronary) supplying blood to the heart.

Causes

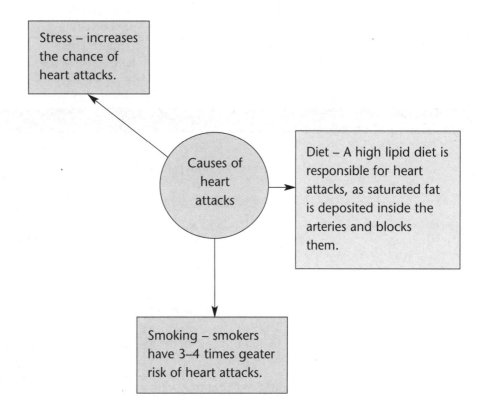

Stress – increases the chance of heart attacks.

Diet – A high lipid diet is responsible for heart attacks, as saturated fat is deposited inside the arteries and blocks them.

Causes of heart attacks

A number of hormones affect heart rate; among these the most important is adrenaline which is secreted from adrenal glands.

Smoking – smokers have 3–4 times geater risk of heart attacks.

Preventive measures

- Regular exercise
- Healthy diet – high fibre diet with less fat. Fats should be unsaturated with less cholesterol
- Life style should be such that one should not feel stressed
- Weight control

Lymphatic System

- This is also a circulatory system
- It brings back the fluid from the body to the blood vessels
- It helps in the production of lymphocytes

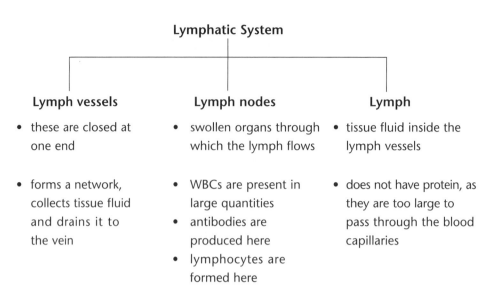

Lymphatic System

Lymph vessels	Lymph nodes	Lymph
• these are closed at one end	• swollen organs through which the lymph flows	• tissue fluid inside the lymph vessels
• forms a network, collects tissue fluid and drains it to the vein	• WBCs are present in large quantities • antibodies are produced here • lymphocytes are formed here	• does not have protein, as they are too large to pass through the blood capillaries

Antibody Production

Germs enter the body; these act as antigens

> Antigens are the substances which are recognised by the body as foreign.

Lymphocytes and the germs come in contact with each other

> Lymphocytes are the WBCs that produce antibodies.

Lymphocytes are activated

> Antibodies are the proteins which are produced by the WBCs in response to antibody stimulation. These destroy antigens. Antibodies are specific. One antibody can destroy only one antigen.

Lymphocytes produce antibodies

> There are two types of lymphocytes – B-lymphocytes which produce antibodies and T-lymphocyte which kill the germ by destroying the cell membrane.

Antibodies combine with germs and destroy them

> Some lymphocytes act as memory cells. These stay in the body long after the infection. They remain in the blood and if the same germ enters the body they produce antibodies rapidly.

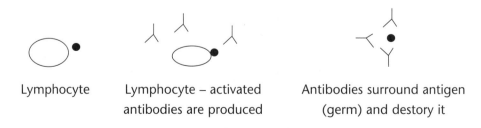

Lymphocyte   Lymphocyte – activated antibodies are produced   Antibodies surround antigen (germ) and destory it

Fig. 2.45 Antibody production and destruction of germs

Phagocytosis

It is a process by which the WBCs attack and kill the germs (pathogens).

WBCs can come out of the blood vessels and kill the germs in the tissues.

WBCs that destroy germs by eating them are known as phagocytes.

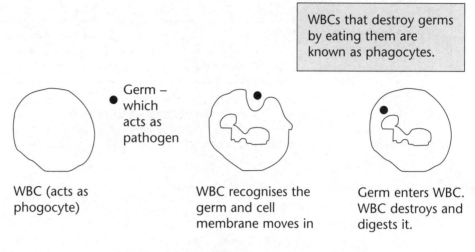

WBC (acts as phogocyte)	WBC recognises the germ and cell membrane moves in	Germ enters WBC. WBC destroys and digests it.

Germ – which acts as pathogen

Fig. 2.46 Process of phagocytosis

Tissue rejection

Donor's tissue is given to the recipient.

Tissues of one individual when transplanted into another are rejected.

This is because the body recognises the tissue as foreign (tissue acts as antigen). This results in the production of antibodies. Antibodies attack the tissue and destroy it.

1. What are the components of blood?
2. What are the functions of blood?
3. Who is known as the universal recipient?
4. Match the following words in the following

Heart	Carriers of oxygen
RBC	Pumping organ
Arteries and veins	Pipes for transport

5. Name the two types of transport system in human beings.
6. What is lymph and state its major functions.
7. Give one major difference between an artery and a vein.
8. What are antigens?

PROGRESS CHECK

8. Antigens are substances which are recognised by the body as foreign substance.
7. An artery carries blood from the heart to the body organs and a vein carries blood from the organs to the heart.
6. Lymph is a light yellow coloured blood plasma which does not contain RBC. It protects the body, helps in removing the waste products, takes part in the digestive process.
5. Blood and lymph.

Arteries and veins	Pipes for transport
RBC	Carriers of oxygen
Heart	Pumping organ

4.
3. A person having a blood group AB.
2. a. Carries carbon dioxide, digested food, hormones, urea to different parts of the body.
   b. Controls body temperature.
1. Plasma, red blood cells, white blood cells, platelets.

2.9 Respiration

After studying this section you will be able to:

● recall that respiration occurs in all living things
● understand that aerobic respiration uses oxygen and is a similar process to burning
● understand that anaerobic respiration does not use oxygen and produces different products
● understand that aerobic respiration releases more energy than anaerobic respiration
● understand what is meant by the term 'oxygen debt'
● define respiration, aerobic respiration and anaerobic respiration
● compare aerobic and anaerobic respiration
● describe the production of lactic acid in the muscles during respiration
● explain respiratory system.

Respiration

Respiration is the process by which chemical energy in sugar molecules is released by oxidation.

2.9.1 Aerobic respiration

Aerobic respiration takes place when glucose reacts completely with oxygen to release energy. Carbon dioxide and water are released as waste products.

> **KEY POINT**
> The equation for respiration is the equation for photosynthesis backwards.

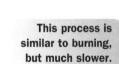
This process is similar to burning, but much slower.

glucose + oxygen ⟶ carbon dioxide + water + energy

$$C_6H_{12}O_6 + 6O_2 \longrightarrow 6CO_2 + 6H_2O + energy \ (38 \ ATPs)$$

Both animals and plants respire all the time. The rate of respiration can be estimated by measuring how much oxygen is used. The heat given off maintains our high body temperature.

Respiration is the process of oxidation or breaking down of organic compounds, particularly simple carbohydrates like glucose, in living cells with the release of energy.

2.9.2 Anaerobic respiration

When glucose is broken down in the complete absence of oxygen, it is called anaerobic respiration. 2 ATPs are produced during anaerobic respiration.

In humans: glucose $\longrightarrow$ lactic acid + **energy**.

$$C_6H_{12}O_6 \xrightarrow{\text{enzymes}} 2C_3H_6O_3 + \text{energy (2 ATP)}$$
Glucose $\qquad\qquad$ lactic acid

In yeast: glucose $\longrightarrow$ carbon dioxide + ethanol + **energy**.

$$C_6H_{12}O_6 \xrightarrow{\text{fermentation}} 2C_2H_5OH + 2CO_2 + \text{(2 ATP)}$$
glucose $\qquad\qquad$ ethanol

Difference between Aerobic and Anaerobic respiration

Aerobic respiration	Anaerobic respiration
takes place in the presence of oxygen	oxygen not required
glucose is broken down into CO_2 and H_2O	CO_2 and C_2H_5OH
$C_6H_{12}O_6 + 6O_2 \longrightarrow 6CO_2 + 6H_2O$	$C_6H_{12}O_6 \longrightarrow C_2H_5OH + CO_2$
38 ATPs are produced	2 ATPs are produced
takes place in the cytoplasm and mitochondria	-only in the cytoplasm

Oxygen debt

Being able to respire without oxygen sounds a great idea.

However, there are two problems:

* anaerobic respiration releases less than half the energy of that released by aerobic respiration
* anaerobic respiration produces lactic acid. Lactic acid causes muscle fatigue.

What causes the oxygen debt?

When vigorous exercise takes place:

* the muscles respire aerobically to release energy
* soon the muscles require more oxygen than can be supplied by the lungs
* the muscles now have to break down glucose without oxygen, using anaerobic respiration
* lactic acid builds up in the muscles
* when the vigorous exercise stops, the lactic acid is still there, and has to be broken down

- this requires oxygen and this 'debt' now has to be repaid
- once we have breathed in enough oxygen to break down the lactic acid, the debt has been repaid.

> **KEY POINT** The fitter we are, the quicker we can breathe in the oxygen, and the sooner we repay the debt.

Role of anaerobic respiration in brewing

Brewing

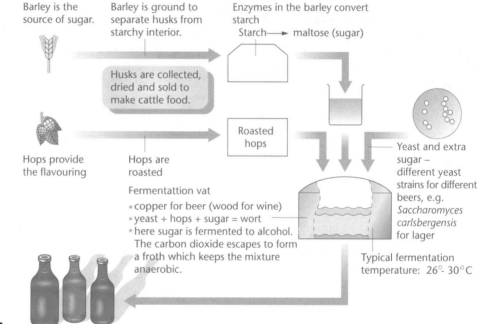

Barley is the source of sugar.

Barley is ground to separate husks from starchy interior.

Husks are collected, dried and sold to make cattle food.

Enzymes in the barley convert starch

Starch ⟶ maltose (sugar)

Roasted hops

Hops provide the flavouring

Hops are roasted

Fermentattion vat
- copper for beer (wood for wine)
- yeast + hops + sugar = wort
- here sugar is fermented to alcohol. The carbon dioxide escapes to form a froth which keeps the mixture anaerobic.

Yeast and extra sugar – different yeast strains for different beers, e.g. *Saccharomyces carlsbergensis* for lager

Typical fermentation temperature: 26°- 30°C

Fig. 2.47

PROGRESS CHECK

1. Write down the equation for aerobic respiration.
2. Write down the equation for anaerobic respiration in humans.
3. State three differences between aerobic and anaerobic respiration.
4. State what instrument can be used to measure the energy content of food.
5. State what is meant by the term 'oxygen debt'?
6. State why fit athletes can repay their oxygen debt more quickly than an unfit person.
7. Place the following structures in order in which air will reach them when breathing in bronchus, trachea, nasal cavity, alveolus.
8. The function of small intestine is to absorb food, the function of lungs is to absorb oxygen. Point out the basic similarities between both the structures that help to speed up the process of absorption.
9. The amount of air moved into or out of the lungs during a single respiratory cycle is the:
   a. respiratory minute volume
   b. tidal volume
   c. residual volume
   d. inspiratory capacity
10. Gas exchange at the respiratory membrane is efficient because:
    a. the differences in partial pressure are substantial
    b. the gases are lipid soluble
    c. the total surface area is large
    d. a, b, and c are correct
11. Why is breathing through the nasal cavity more desirable than breathing through the mouth?
12. Explain why carbon monoxide is toxic.

1. $C_6H_{12}O_6 + 6O_2 = 6CO_2 + 6H_2O +$ energy; 2. Glucose ⟶ lactic acid + energy; 3. Aerobic – uses oxygen, more efficient, does not produce lactic acid; 4. Calorimeter; 5. Anaerobic respiration produces lactic acid. This has to be broken down by oxygen when exercise stops. The oxygen that is breathed in after exercise repays this debt; 6. Athletes usually have bigger, more powerful lungs that can absorb oxygen faster than the lungs of an unfit person. 7. nasal cavity, trachea, bronchus, alveolus; 8. Moist surface, large surface area, thin membrane, rich blood supply. 9. b. tidal volume 10. a. the differences in partial pressure are substantial 11. Nasal passage filters the air of any dust particles and germs, maintains the moisture and temperature of the air inhaled. 12. Carbon monoxide combines with oxygen in the blood to form carboxy haemoglobin which does not allow any more absorption of oxygen. So this leads to starvation of oxygen in the cell.

2.9.3 Gaseous exchange

LEARNING SUMMARY

After studying this section you should be able to:

● *explain how air is drawn into and forced out of the lungs*
● *state the composition of the inhaled and exhaled air*
● *explain how the lungs are adapted for gaseous exchange*
● *list the features of gaseous exchange surfaces in animals*
● *state the differences in composition between inspired and expired air*
● *describe a test for carbon dioxide*
● *describe the effects of physical activity on rate and depth of breathing*
● *describe the effects of tobacco smoke on the respiratory system.*

Exchanging air

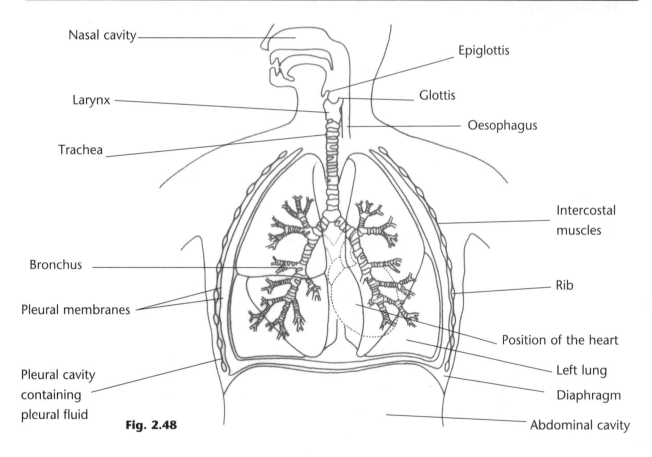

Fig. 2.48

Gaseous exchange depends upon diffusion. For efficient diffusion the surface should have the following characters:

- thin – a single cell lining
- close to the transport system
- moist – allows gases to dissolve
- large surface area
- have a concentration gradient – achieved by the movement of air and the transport or use of the gas.

> **KEY POINT** Breathing is a set of muscular movements that draw air in and out of the lungs. It means that more oxygen is available in the lungs and more carbon dioxide can be removed.

Drawing air in and out of the lungs involves changes in pressure and volume in the chest. These changes work because the **pleural** membranes form an airtight **pleural cavity**.

Breathing is needed in large or very active animals because they need more oxygen.

> **KEY POINT** The pleural cavity is airtight and so an increase in volume in the cavity will decrease the pressure.

Role of ribs

Common mistake: the lungs do not force the ribs outwards. When the ribs move this causes the lungs to inflate.

inhalation

1. Two sets of intercostal muscles are attached to the ribs. They are antagonistic.

2. Wheir the external inter costal muscles contract they move the rib cage upwards and outwards increasing the volume in the thorax.

3. Diaphragm contracts, moves down increasing the volume of the thorax.

4. Increased volume reduces the air pressure in the thorax.

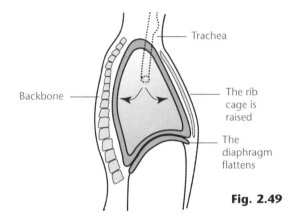

Fig. 2.49

Exhalation

1. Exactly opposite phenomena happen.

2. Decrease in the thoracic volume.

3. Increased air pressure.

4. Air is expelled out.

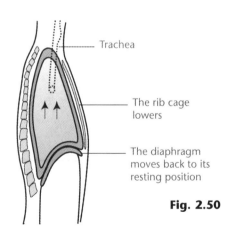

Fig. 2.50

Whilst the air is in the lungs, the proportions of oxygen and carbon dioxide are changed.

There is still 17% oxygen in air that is breathed out. This makes artificial respiration possible.

Gas	Percentage of the gas present in	
	air breathed in	air breathed out
carbon dioxide	0.04	4
oxygen	21	17
nitrogen	78	78
water vapour	low	high

Testing for carbon dioxide.

Two chemical reagents can be used to test for carbon dioxide. They change colour when the gas is passed through them

Lime water – colourless to milky

Hydrogen carbonate – red to yellow.

> **KEY POINT** **Gaseous exchange occurs when oxygen diffuses from the air into the bloodstream and carbon dioxide diffuses the other way.**

Gaseous exchange occurs in the millions of air sacs in the lungs. These are called **alveoli**. The structure of these alveoli makes them very efficient (well adapted) for gaseous exchange.

Remember: deoxygenated blood is not really blue!

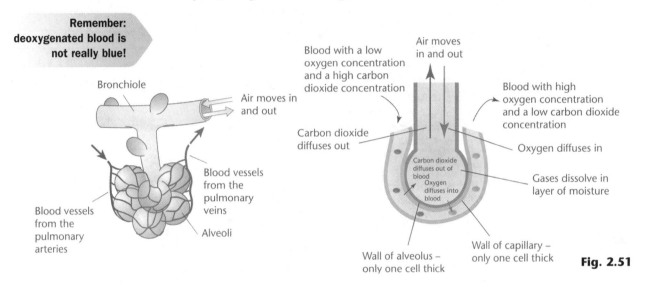

Fig. 2.51

The adaptations of lungs are:

The leaves of plants are also adapted for gaseous exchange.

● millions of alveoli provide a surface area of about 90 m²
● numerous blood vessels provide a rich blood supply
● the alveoli have a thin film of moisture, so that the gases can dissolve
● the blood and air are separated by only two layers of cells.

Breathing rate ⟶ increases with physical activity

so more energy is required

so more oxygen is required

Effects of tobacco smoke on the respiratory system

Chemical	harmful effects on respiratory system
Carbon monoxide	poisonous gas. It combines with haemoglobin preventing the transport of oxygen
Nicotine	harmful effects on heart and acts as a carcinogen
Smoke particles	irritate the air passages, causing inflammation, increased mucus production, resulting in chronic bronchitis. Coughing and the presence of particles in the alveoli can lead to emphysema
Tar	a carcinogen which increases the risk of lung cancer. Lines the air passages, increasing mucus production and paralysing and damaging cilia causing bronchitis.

PROGRESS CHECK

1. Why does an elephant need to breathe more whilst a tree, of the same size, does not?
2. Which two structures contract to make a person breathe in?
3. What is the difference between the oxygen content of air that is breathed in compared to air that is breathed out?
4. Where does blood go after it has been through the lungs and how does it get there?
5. What is the advantage of moist, ciliated mucus membrane in the nasal passage?
6. Describe the path of air on the way to lungs.
7. What is the effect of smoke particles on the breathing system?
8. What happens to breathing rate after physical exercise?
9. What should be the characteristics of breathing surfaces?

9. Moist, large surface area, thin membrane, difference in concentration gradient.
8. Breathing rate would increase after physical exercise because muscles would need more oxygen so more blood has to be pumped through the body.
7. The particles of smoke irritate the air passages, causing inflammation, increased production of mucus.
6. Air enters the nostrils, passes through the trachea, bronchus into the lungs.
5. When air passes through the nasal passage the air is filtered of bacteria and dust particles, it also controls the temperature and moisture of the air inhaled.
4. It goes back to the left atrium of the heart through the pulmonary vein.
3. 21% – 17% = 4%;
2. The intercostal muscles and the diaphragm;
1. An elephant is more active and so needs more oxygen;

2.10 Excretion

The student should be able to :

- *define excretion*
- *describe the function of the kidney*
- *describe the urinary system and its organs*
- *explain the formation of urea and the breakdown of alcohol, drugs and hormones in the liver*
- *explain dialysis and discuss its application*
- *explain how a kidney transplant is performed.*

Definition – Excretion is defined as the removal of toxic waste products of metabolism and substances of excess requirement from an organism.

Significance of excretion

- Removal of metabolic wastes
- Removal of unwanted by-products
- Regulation of ionic concentration of body fluids
- Regulation of water content of the body
- Regulation of pH.

Excretion in Humans

1. Skin: water, nail, lactic acid, CO_2, ammonia traces of vitamin B and C
2. Lungs: CO_2 and H_2O
3. Liver: bile pigments, toxins, urine
4. Kidney: water, urea, uric acid, salt of Na, K, Ca, Mg

If the wastes are retained in the body they become toxic.

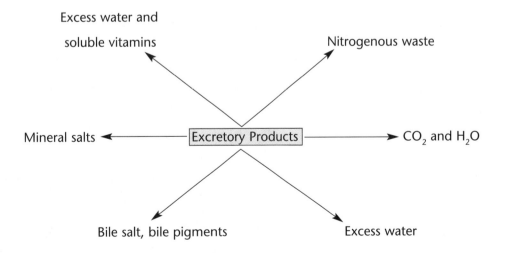

There are two kidneys, if one fails the other can still carry on the normal function of excretion and osmoregulation.

Each kidney is divided into following four parts.

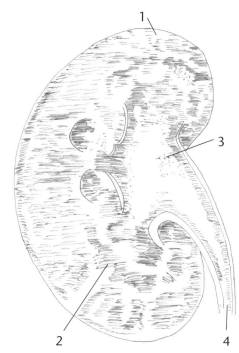

1. **Cortex** – this layer is jam-packed with millions of nephrons. The cortex acts as the filtering layer of the kidney.

2. **Medulla**– the middle layer. Tubes carrying filtered wastes travel from the cortex through the medulla towards the pelvis.

3. **Pelvis** – this is the area where all the collecting tubules come together and connect with the ureter.

4. **Ureter** – transports the wastes (urine) into the urinary bladder.

Fig. 2.52

Nephron: The structural units of the kidney. Each kidney consists of about a million, long, coiled, fine tubules.

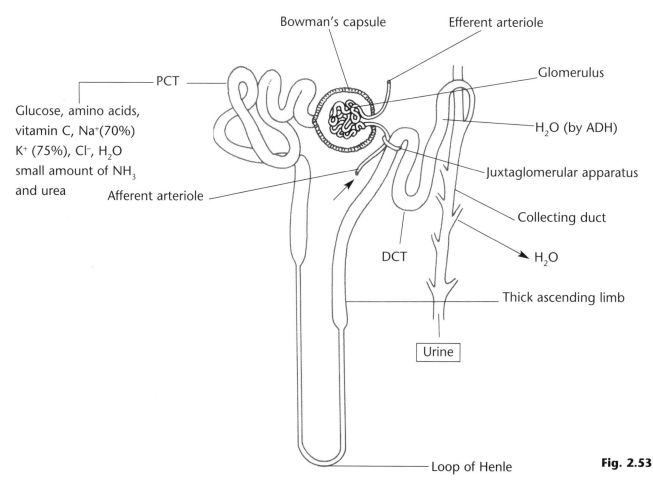

Fig. 2.53

Diagram of excretory system

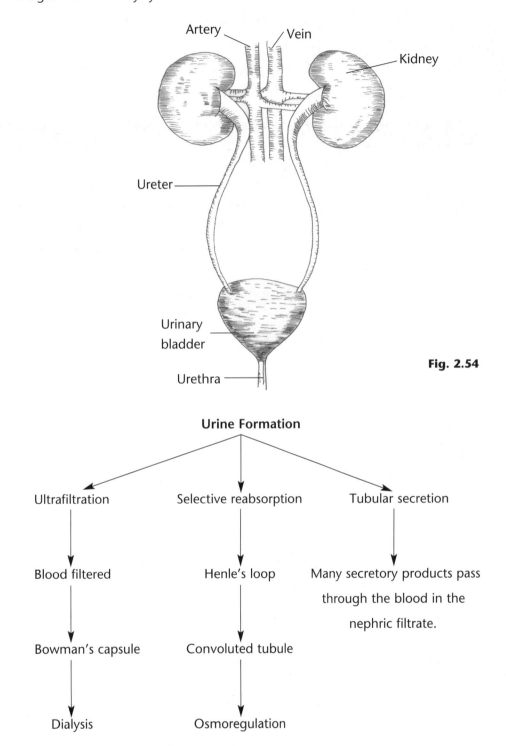

Fig. 2.54

Urine Formation

Ultrafiltration — Selective reabsorption — Tubular secretion

Blood filtered — Henle's loop — Many secretory products pass through the blood in the nephric filtrate.

Bowman's capsule — Convoluted tubule

Dialysis — Osmoregulation

Composition of urine

1. Water : 900–950 cc/litre
2. Urea : 25 g
3. NaCl : 9.0 g
4. KCl : 2.5 g

5. Creatinine : 1.0 g

6. Uric acid : 0.6 g

7. Ammonia : 0.7 g

8. Ca + Mg : 0.4 g

The kidneys – control of waste

> **KEY POINT** It is the job of the kidneys to filter urea from the blood.

Urea is a waste material produced from the breakdown of proteins.

The kidney has thousands of fine **tubules**, called **nephrons**.

Blood capillaries carry blood at **high pressure** into these tubules. The small molecules in the blood are squeezed out of the capillaries and collected by the tubules. This is called **ultrafiltration**.

Fig. 2.55

The small molecules that are filtered out include:

water   glucose   salt   urea

> If all of this fluid reached the bladder, the whole day would be spent on drinking water.

The body cannot afford to lose all of this glucose, salt and water. So these molecules are **reabsorbed** back into the blood, leaving just a little water and all of the urea to continue on to the bladder. This liquid is called urine.

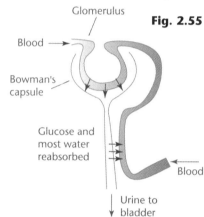

> **KEY POINT** Urea is made in the liver from excess protein.

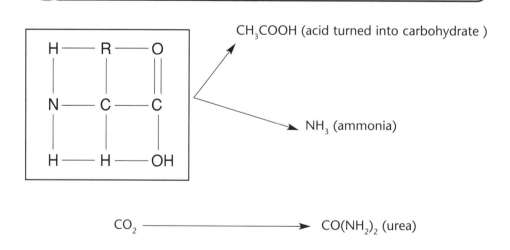

This urea is dissolved in blood plasma filtered in the kidneys and excreted.

Kidney tubules

The kidney works by filtering the blood under pressure and then reabsorbing the useful substances back into the blood. This all occurs in nephrons.

If the blood pressure drops too much then the filtration may stop.

Selective reabsorption of glucose and amino acids occurs by active transport.

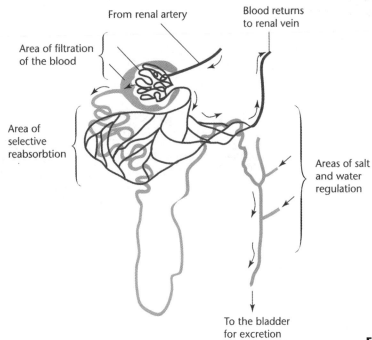

Fig. 2.56

> **KEY POINT**
> The nephron has three main areas, a filter unit, an area of selective reabsorption and an area for salt and water regulation.

How the nephron changes the composition of the fluid is shown in the table:

Exam questions often ask for an explanation of the zero figures in this table.

substance	Percentage of substance in		
	blood plasma	filtered fluid	urine
water	90	99	97
proteins	9	0	0
glucose	0.1	0.1	0
urea	0.03	0.03	2.0

- Protein is absent from the urine because the molecules are too large to pass through the filter unit and so stay in the blood.

- Glucose is absent from the urine because it is selectively reabsorbed from the tubule back into the blood.

Treating kidney disease

People may suffer from kidney failure for a number of reasons. A person can survive if half of their nephrons are still working but if the situation worsens then there are two options:

> A person can therefore survive with one working kidney.

Kidney failure

Kidney dialysis   Kidney transplant

Kidney dialysis

> **KEY POINT** Kidney dialysis involves linking the person up to a dialysis machine. This takes over the role of the kidneys and removes waste substances from the blood.

> The anticoagulant stops the blood clotting while it is in the machine.

> The bubble trap stops bubbles of air entering the body in the blood.

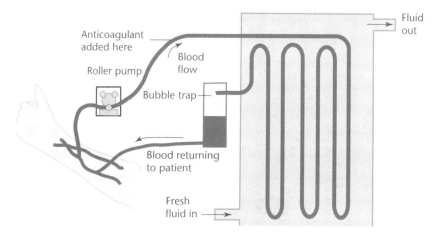

Fig. 2.57

The blood is removed from a vein in the arm. It then passes through a long coiled tube made of partially permeable cellophane. The fluid surrounding the tube contains water, salts, glucose and amino acids but no waste materials, such as urea. These waste materials therefore diffuse out of the blood into the fluid.

Transplants

> Over 2000 kidney transplants are carried out in UK every year but donors are in short supply.

As a person can survive with one kidney, it is possible for a person to donate one kidney to be transplanted into another person.

> **KEY POINT** The main problem with transplants is to prevent the person's immune system rejecting the transplanted kidney.

This is avoided by taking certain precautions:

● making sure that the donor has a similar 'tissue type' to the patient

● treating the patient with drugs or radiation to make their immune system less effective.

Liver functions

Excretory function	Some proteins and other nitrogenous compounds are broken down in the liver by a process called deamination. As a result of these reactions, a nitrogenous waste called urea is formed.
Digestive function	The liver produces bile, which is temporarily stored in the gall bladder before being released into the small intestine where it helps "emulsify" (break down) lipid molecules.
Role in circulatory system	The liver removes and breaks down old red blood cells. It is also responsible for maintaining "normal" levels of glucose in the blood. When stimulated by insulin, the liver removes glucose from the blood and converts it into glycogen for storage. When stimulated by the hormone glucagon, the liver does the opposite; it breaks down glycogen, producing glucose, which is released into the bloodstream. The liver is also responsible for removing potentially hazardous chemicals from the blood. It "detoxifies" the blood. Alcoholics and other types of addicts are more vulnerable to liver disease because alcohol and other drugs, while passing through the liver, damage it.

PROGRESS CHECK

1. The kidneys have a high rate of respiration. Why is this?
2. Why might too much salt in the diet harm the kidneys?
3. Why do patients who have received transplant kidneys have to be kept in a sterile environment for some time after the operation?

1. Energy is needed because selective reabsorption is by active transport. 2. High salt may cause high blood pressure and high blood pressure may damage the delicate nephrons. 3. The patient is susceptible to microbes because their immune system has been weakened.

PROGRESS CHECK

1. Which of these is not a function of kidneys?
    a. Maintenance of acid base balance
    b. Excretion of nitrogenous waste products
    c. Temperature regulation
    d. Maintenance of water balance

2. Which of these is not a normal constituent of urine: sugar, urea or creatinine?

3. Label the parts of a neuron.

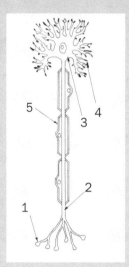

1. _____

2. _____

3. _____

4. _____

5. _____

4. Label the parts of the eye.

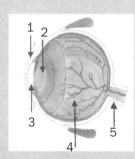

1. _____

2. _____

3. _____

4. _____

5. _____

5. Which is the correct pathway for the elimination of urine?
    a. urethra, ureter, bladder, kidney
    b. kidneys, urethra, bladder, ureter
    c. bladder, ureters, kidney, urethra
    d. kidneys, ureters, bladder, urethra

6. In humans, for carbon dioxide to be excreted, it must pass from the blood into:
    a. nephrons
    b. alveoli
    c. sweat glands
    d. liver

7. Which is not a metabolic waste in humans?
    a. carbon dioxide
    b. oxygen
    c. salt
    d. urea
    e. water

8. Use the diagram to answer the following questions.
   i. The structural unit shown in the diagram is called:
      a. an alveolus
      b. a nephron
      c. a sweat gland
      d. a ureter
   ii. Into which structure does the filtrate first pass?
      a. 1   b. 2
      c. 3   d. 5
   iii. In which area are materials needed by the body reabsorbed?
      a. 2   b. 3
      c. 4   d. 5
   iv. In which area is urine collected?
      a. 2   b. 3
      c. 4   d. 5
   v. Which of the following does not normally enter structure 3?
      a. salts
      b. red blood cells
      c. urea
      d. water
      e. glucose
   vi. Which structure is the glomerulus?
   vii. Which structure is the loop of Henle?
   viii. Which structure is the collecting tubule?
   ix. Which structure is the Bowman's Capsule?

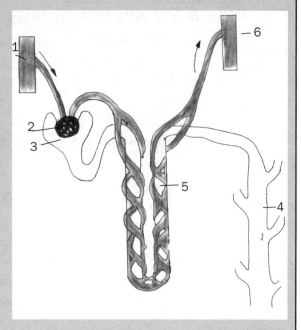

8.
i. b   ii. 2   iii. 5   iv. c   v. b   vi. 2   vii. 5   viii. 4   ix. 3

5. d   6. b   7. a

4.
1. conjunctiva   2. lens   3. aqueous humour   4. vitrious humour   5. optic nerve

3.
1. dendrite   2. axon   3. cell body   4. dendrites   5. myelin sheath

1. a   2. sugar

2.11 Coordination and response

LEARNING SUMMARY

After studying this section you should be able to:

- *understand the role played by hormones in plants and animals*
- *describe nervous control in the human body*
- *define sense organs as groups of receptor cells responding to specific stimuli*
- *define homeostasis as the maintenance of a constant internal environment*
- *describe the effects of alcohol and drugs and dangers of their misuse.*

2.11.1 Plant hormones

LEARNING SUMMARY

After studying this section you should be able to:

- *explain what a hormone is and know where they are produced in the body*
- *understand the role of hormones in a plant body.*

What is a hormone?

KEY POINT

A hormone is a chemical messenger in the body. They are released by glands and travel in the bloodstream to reach their target organ.

Basic characteristics of hormones

1. secreted by ductless glands, released into the blood directly

2. transported to the target organs by blood

3. required in small amounts, but are very active

4. specific in their action

5. excess or deficiency of a hormone produces serious consequences.

Control of plant growth

Just like humans, plants also respond to a stimulus, although much more slowly. They do it by growing towards or away from the stimulus:

- **phototropism** – shoots respond to light by growing towards it
- **geotropism** – shoots grow away from gravity, roots grow towards it
- **hydrotropism** – roots grow towards water

KEY POINT

Auxins are plant growth hormones.

Function of Auxins

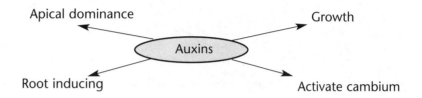

Plant movements can be categorised into two types:

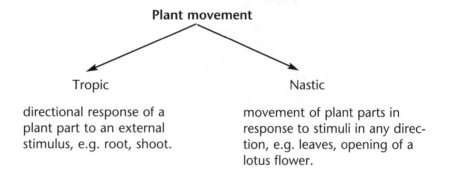

Plant movement

Tropic

directional response of a plant part to an external stimulus, e.g. root, shoot.

Nastic

movement of plant parts in response to stimuli in any direction, e.g. leaves, opening of a lotus flower.

How auxins work

Auxins make cells grow longer.

Fig. 2.58

Shoots grow towards the light because auxins collect on the dark side of the shoot. This causes the cells on the dark side to lengthen.

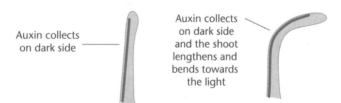

Auxin collects on dark side

Auxin collects on dark side and the shoot lengthens and bends towards the light

Fig. 2.59

Other uses of plant growth hormones:

- hormone rooting powder promotes the growth of roots in shoot cuttings
- unpollinated flowers can be treated to produce seedless fruits
- ripening of fruits can be slowed down in order to keep them fresh during transport to consumers
- some weed killers contain a synthetic hormone which causes broad leaf plants to 'outgrow' themselves and die.

These techniques are often used by commercial growers to increase their productivity.

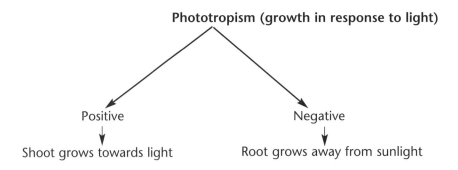

Phototropism

Plant growth in response to light.

When a shoot is exposed to light, from one side the auxins get destroyed causing unequal distribution of auxins which leads to unequal growth and bending of the stem.

Geotropism

Plant growth in response to gravity.

Auxins are attracted by the gravity, so they help the plant parts grow towards the earth.

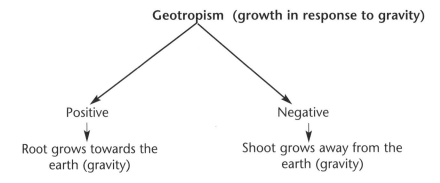

Synthetic plant hormones used as weed killers

● Synthetic plant hormones are chemicals similar to auxins.

● If used or sprayed, it results in uncontrolled growth leading to death of the unwanted plant.

● Some plant hormones are successively used to kill commonly found weeds.

1. What are the function of auxins?
2. Differentiate between tropic and nastic movements.
3. What do you understand by phototropic and geotropic movements?

1. Helps in growth, elongation, enlargement, promotes cell division during growing season for the shoots and the roots, promotes flowering.
2. The movement of a plant in a particular direction in response to a stimulus is called tropic and when there is no direction of movement it is nastic movement.
3. Photo – movement in response to light. Geo – earth/gravity movement towards/away from the earth.

2.11.2 Animal Hormones

 LEARNING SUMMARY

After studying this section you should be able to:
- *name the important hormones synthesised in our body*
- *explain the role of adrenalin as an emergency hormone.*

Hormone producing glands are called endocrine glands.

During pregnancy the placenta also makes hormones.

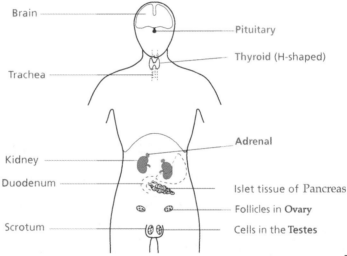

Fig. 2.60

The diagram shows the main hormone-producing glands of the body. Between them they make a number of different hormones:

Gland	hormones produced	action
Pituitary	Anti-diuretic hormone (ADH)	• Water balance
	Luteinising hormone (LH)	• Ovulation and progesterone production
	Follicle stimulating hormone (FSH)	• Growth of a follicle
Thyroid	Thyroxine	• Controls metabolic rate
Adrenal	Adrenaline	• Prepares the body for action
Pancreas	Insulin	• Control of blood glucose level
Ovary	Estrogen	• Controls puberty and menstrual cycle in the female
	Progesterone	• Maintains pregnancy
Testis	Testosterone	• Controls puberty in the male

Role of Adrenalin

Adrenalin gland

(situated above the kidneys)

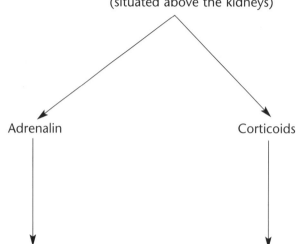

Adrenalin

1. required at the time of emergency to face physical or emotional stress
2. increases metabolism
3. releases more energy
4. increases blood supply to muscles

Corticoids

1. regulate carbohydrate, fats and proteins
2. stimulate kidneys to retain Na^+ and secrete K^+
3. influence the functioning of sex organs and accessory sexual characteristics

In response to Adrenalin:

● heart beats faster and supplies oxygen to brain and muscles beat faster

● blood vessels in the skin and the digestive system become narrow and so less blood flows through here and more blood is directed to the brain and muscles

● liver breaks down glycogen and releases glucose into the blood which ultimately provides energy.

1. Which hormone is secreted by the adrenal cortex and the adrenal glands?
2. Which hormone is described as the emergency hormone and why?

 PROGRESS CHECK

1. Corticoids, adrenalin.

2. Adrenalin is considered as the emergency hormone as it prepares the body for emergency situations like emotional stress, fear, etc.

2.11.3 Nervous control in human

LEARNING SUMMARY

After studying this section you should be able to:

● **explain how organisms respond to stimuli**
● **explain how the eye works**
● **describe the nerve pathway of a reflex**
● **define hormone, sense organ**
● **describe the chemical control of metabolic activity by adrenalin**
● **describe the human nervous system**
● **identify sensory and motor neurons**

Responding to stimuli

Hormone – A chemical secreted by an endocrine gland. It is transported in the blood stream and usually has a long-term effect on a target organ.

Sense organ – A group of receptor cells responding to a specific stimulus, such as light, sound, touch, temperature, chemicals.

KEY POINT

All living organisms can respond to changes in the environment. This is called sensitivity. Plants usually respond more slowly than animals.

Although the speed and type of response may be very different, the order of events is always the same:

Nerves carry messages quicker than hormones.

stimulus	receptor	co-ordination	effector	response
light, sound, smell, taste or touch	detects the stimulus	usually carried out by the brain or spinal cord	most often a muscle or gland	for example, movement

The **receptors** detect the changes and pass information on to the **central nervous system** (the brain and spinal cord). This coordinates all the information and sends a message to the **effectors** to bring about a response. All these messages are sent by nerves or hormones.

Receptors

KEY POINT

The job of receptors is to detect the stimulus and send information about it to the central nervous system.

Human nervous system is made up of two parts:

- **central nervous system**, i.e., brain, spinal cord
- **peripheral nervous system**

The brain coordinates the body's responses to stimuli.

Central Nervous System (CNS)

Brain, spinal cord which control all the other organs of the body.

Peripheral Nervous System (PNS)

Nerves which connect all parts of the body to the central nervous system.

Sence organs are connected to PNS.

The different receptors in the human body respond to different stimuli:

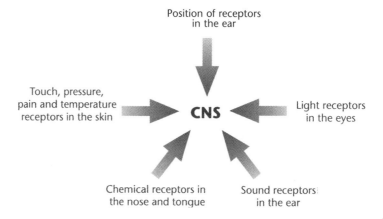

Fig. 2.61

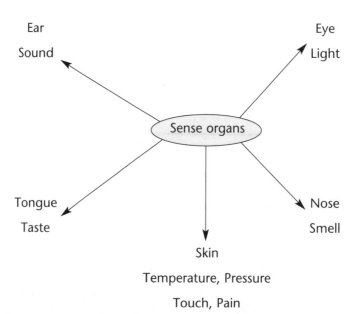

> **KEY POINT** The receptors are often gathered together into sense organs. They have various other structures that help the receptors to gain the maximum amount of information.

One of these sense organs is the eye:

Learn this diagram and how to label it.

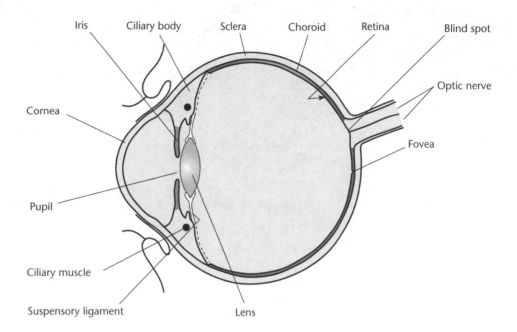

Fig. 2.62

The light enters through the **pupil**. It is focused onto the **retina** by the **cornea** and the **lens**.

The size of the pupil can be changed by the muscles of the iris when the brightness of the light changes. This tries to make sure that the same amount of light enters the eye.

Try this by looking in a mirror and turning on and off the light.

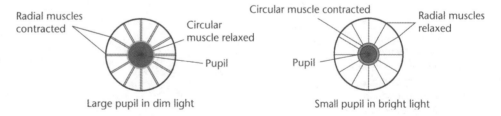

Fig. 2.63

The job of the lens is to change shape so that the image is always focused on the light sensitive retina.

KEY POINT To change from looking at a distant object to a near object, the lens has to become more rounded and powerful. This is called *accommodation*.

Remember that the ciliary muscles contract to allow the lens to focus upon a near object.

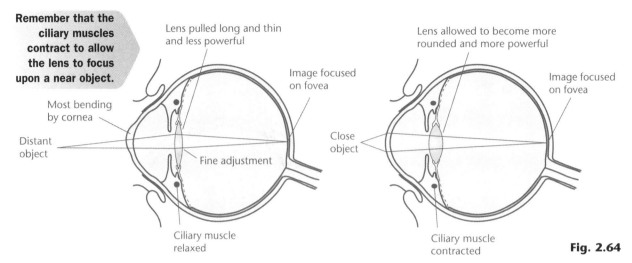

Fig. 2.64

The receptors are cells in the retina called **rods** and **cones**. They detect light and send messages to the brain along the optic nerve. The rods and cones do slightly different jobs.

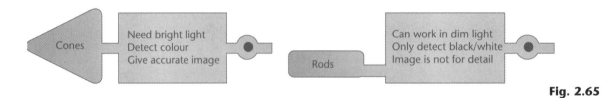

Fig. 2.65

Neurones and responses

KEY POINT Neurones are specialised cells that carry messages around the body in the form of electrical charges.

There are three main types:

- **sensory neurones** – they carry electrical messages from the sense organs to the CNS

Don't get confused between nerves and neurones. Nerves are collections of thousands of neurones.

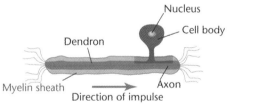

Fig. 2.66

- **motor neurones** – they carry electrical messages from the CNS to the effectors, such as muscles and glands

Make sure that you can put arrows on the neurones to show the direction of the impulse.

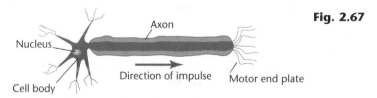

Fig. 2.67

- **relay neurones** – they relay messages between neurones in the CNS.

One neurone does not directly connect with another. The projections at the ends of the neurones end just short of the next neurone. This leaves a small gap.

Many of the drugs mentioned in section 2.8 affect synapses.

> **KEY POINT**
> The junction between two neurones is called a synapse and messages are passed across by chemical transmitter molecules.

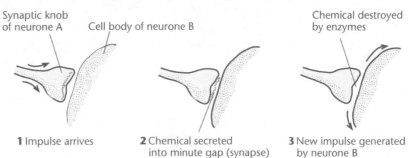

Synaptic knob of neurone A Cell body of neurone B

Chemical destroyed by enzymes

1 Impulse arrives

2 Chemical secreted into minute gap (synapse)

3 New impulse generated by neurone B

Fig. 2.68

Once the information reaches the CNS from a sensory neurone there is a choice:

A. the message can be sent to the higher centres of the brain and the organism might decide to make a response. This is called a **voluntary action**

B. the message may be passed straight to a motor neurone via a relay neurone. This is much quicker and is called a **reflex action**.

Don't say that reflexes happen unconsciously!

A reflex action	A voluntary action
Very quick, so protects the body	Takes longer time
Does not necessarily involve the brain	Always involves the brain
Does not involve conscious thought	Involves conscious thought

> **KEY POINT**
> A reflex is a rapid response that does not involve conscious thought. It protects the body from damage.

Path of reflex action

In the withdrawal reflex, pain on the skin is the stimulus. The response is the muscle moving the part of the body away from danger.

1. Stimulus is detected by sensory cell.

2. Impulse passes down sensory neurone.

3. Relay neurone passes impulse to motor neurone.

4. Motor neurone passes impulse to effector.

5. Muscle contracts.

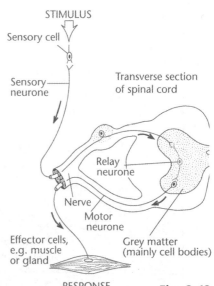

STIMULUS

Sensory cell

Sensory neurone

Transverse section of spinal cord

Relay neurone

Nerve

Motor neurone

Effector cells, e.g. muscle or gland

Grey matter (mainly cell bodies)

RESPONSE

Fig. 2.69

Reflex actions are not co-ordinated by the brain although, in most cases, the brain is immediately aware that the reflex action has taken place.

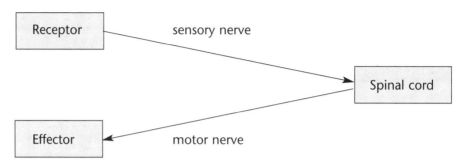

Effectors – muscles or glands which respond when they receive impulses from motor neurons, e.g. biceps and triceps.

PROGRESS CHECK

1. What is the job of receptors?
2. What do receptors in the skin detect?
3. How is the shape of the lens in the eye made more rounded?
4. What is the CNS?
5. Name two types of effector organs in the body.
6. Muscles are formed from cells which have the special property of being able to
    _____.
7. Nerve cells are specialised cells. Suggest how the following parts of the nerve cell enable the cell to function successfully: cytoplasm, myelin sheath.
8. Reflex involves a response to a stimulus.
    Complete the following flow chart by putting the following terms in the boxes to show the correct sequence in a reflex.
    coordinator, effector, receptor, response, stimulus

9. The human nervous system is divided into two major divisions, list them:

    A. _____

    B. _____

10. What are the four functions of the nervous system?

1. Receptors detect stimuli and pass information on to sensory neurones as electrical impulses; 2. Touch, pressure, pain, temperature; 3. The ciliary muscle contracts, loosening the suspensory ligaments; 4. The central nervous system, it is made up of the brain and spinal cord; 5. Muscles and glands; 6. Contract; 7. Cytoplasm – helps to conduct electrical impulses; myelin sheath – prevents the impulses passing out of the axon; 8. stimulus, receptor, coordinator, effector, response; 9. Central nervous system, peripheral nervous system.
10. a. Controls and regulates all voluntary muscular activities of different parts of the body.
b. Regulates involuntary activities of respiratory organs, etc.
c. Coordinates working of various glands and tissues of the body.
d. keeps us informed about changes in the external and internal environment through sense organs.

2.11.4 Homeostasis

After studying this section you will be able to:
● **recall that homeostasis is maintaining a constant internal environment**
● **understand how the kidney controls the urea and water level of the body**
● **understand how the body controls its own temperature.**

Definition of homeostasis

Maintenance of temperature, water content and concentration of glucose in the cells is called homeostasis.

Blood glucose

It is vital that the glucose level in the blood is kept constant. If not controlled, it would **rise** after eating and **fall** when hungry. **Insulin** is the hormone that controls the level of glucose in the blood.

glucose in the blood → **insulin** → Glycogen in the liver

Fig. 2.70

Remember: glucose is used for respiration to release energy.

KEY POINT Insulin converts excess glucose into glycogen to be stored in the liver.

Diabetics do not produce enough insulin naturally. They need regular insulin injections in order to control the level of glucose in their blood.

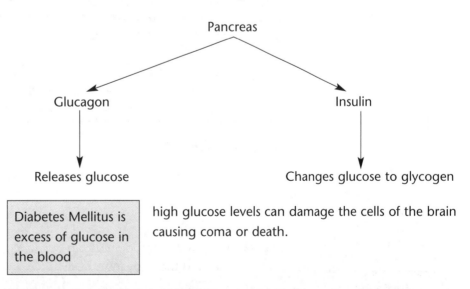

Pancreas

Glucagon   Insulin

Releases glucose   Changes glucose to glycogen

Diabetes Mellitus is excess of glucose in the blood

high glucose levels can damage the cells of the brain causing coma or death.

KEY POINT Healthy people have no glucose in their urine – a test for diabetes.

The kidneys – control of water

The kidneys also control the amount of water in our bodies.

Our bodies get water from:

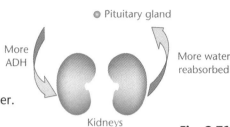

Fig. 2.71

- the food we eat
- the liquids we drink
- water produced by respiration

Sometimes we do not have enough water.

Too thirsty?

- the pituitary gland produces more of the hormone called ADH
- this causes the tubules to reabsorb more water
- the urine becomes more concentrated, and the body saves water.

Sometimes we drink too much liquid. Then the opposite happens.

> Try to think of the body as a container full of liquid. The more water you put in, the more will overflow.

Drunk too much liquid?

- Less ADH is produced.
- The kidney tubules reabsorb less water.
- More water reaches the bladder.
- Large amounts of dilute urine is produced.

Temperature control

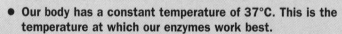

> **KEY POINT**
> - Our body has a constant temperature of 37°C. This is the temperature at which our enzymes work best.
> - The average room temperature is about 20°C.
> - This means we are always warmer than our surroundings.
> - We are constantly losing heat to our surroundings.
> - We produce the heat from respiration.
> - Core body temperature is monitored and controlled by the brain.
> - Temperature receptors send nerve impulses to the skin.
> - It is the job of the skin to regulate our body temperature.

When we feel too hot

We feel hot when we need to lose heat faster, as our core body temperature is in danger of rising.

> Common error:
> Some students lose marks in exams because they say that blood vessels move away from the surface of the skin. Blood vessels cannot move.

We do this by:

- **sweating** – as water evaporates from our skin, it absorbs heat energy. This cools the skin and the body loses heat.
- **vasodilation** – blood capillaries near the skin surface get wider to allow more blood to flow near the surface. Because the blood is warmer than the air, it cools down and the body loses more heat.

When we feel too cold

When we feel too cold we are in danger of losing heat too quickly and cooling down. This means we need to conserve our heat to maintain a constant 37°C.

We do this by:

- **shivering** – rapid contraction and relaxation of body muscles. This increases the rate of respiration and more energy is released as heat

- **vasoconstriction** – blood capillaries near the skin surface get narrower and this process reduces blood flow to the surface. The blood is diverted to deeper within the body to conserve heat.

1. State which hormone converts glucose in the blood into glycogen in the liver.
2. State four small molecules that are filtered from the blood by ultrafiltration.
3. State which of these molecules are not reabsorbed.
4. Explain how the hormone called ADH controls the body's water level.
5. Explain what happens in the skin when we feel too hot.

1. Insulin; 2. Salt, water, glucose, urea; 3. Urea; 4. When thirsty, increased levels of ADH cause more water to be reabsorbed back into the blood. The opposite happens when we drink too much; 5. Sweating causes heat to be lost as the sweat evaporates. Vasodilation of surface capillaries allow more blood to flow near skin surface, thus allowing the blood to cool down.

Role of hormones in homeostasis

1. **Control of endocrine glands by hormones**

   Hypothalamus produces releasing hormone in response to some external stimulus

   Stimulates thyroid gland to produce thyroxin

   If the level of thyroxin in the blood is

   high   low

   releases less amount of   releases more amount of
   releasing hormone   releasing hormone

2. **Control of metabolites**

   Levels of metabolites control the secretion of certain hormones.

   e.g. after a meal the glucose level in blood rises, which stimulates the secretion of insulin to act on it. With the fall of glucose level in the blood decrease of insulin level takes place.

Negative feedback effect

- If the level of thyroxin in blood is high it exerts a negative feedback effect on the hypothalamus and anterior pituitary.

- These now secrete less amount of releasing hormone and thyroid stimulating hormone respectively.

2.11.5 Drugs

Alcohol

Alcohol is the most widely abused drug in the world today. While there are many types of alcohol, the type that is found in drinks and medicines is known as 'ethyl alcohol' or ethanol.

Effects of alcohol

- Blurred vision
- Slowed heart rate, reduced blood pressure
- Death from respiratory arrest
- Liver damage

Heroin

Heroin is a highly addictive drug derived from morphine, a naturally occurring substance extracted from the seed pod of certain varieties of poppy plants.

Effects of heroin

- Addiction
- Infectious diseases (e.g., HIV/AIDS and hepatitis B and C)
- Infection of heart lining and valves

Regular consumption of drugs like alcohol and heroin can lead to social problems like crime. Balanced family relationships, which are the basis of most social structures may also become disturbed.

Sample IGCSE questions

1. (a) Dick was running the 5000m in his school's sports day. He noticed that after a few seconds his heart was beating faster. Explain why his heart beat increased as he started to run. **[3]**

> To pump more blood to the muscles ✓ so that they could get more oxygen ✓ and glucose ✓.

(b) He also noticed that as he ran his breathing rate increased. Explain why Dick breathed faster. **[3]**

> To absorb more oxygen ✓ for respiration ✓ and to get rid of excess carbon dioxide ✓.

(c) Complete the following equation to show how Dick was supplying his muscles with energy. **[2]**

$$C_6H_{12}O_6 + 6O_2 \longrightarrow 6H_2O + 6CO_2 ✓ ✓$$

(d) After a couple of minutes Dick's muscles started to run short of oxygen. They broke down the glucose without oxygen. State what this type of respiration is called. **[1]**

> Anaerobic ✓.

(e) Complete the word equation to show what was happening in Dick's muscles. **[1]**

> Glucose ⟶ lactic acid ✓.

(f) When the race was over Dick noticed that he was still out of breath even though he had stopped running. Explain why Dick was still panting. **[3]**

> Lactic acid had built up in his muscles ✓. It is toxic and must be broken down ✓. Oxygen is required for this and Dick continues to pant until he has absorbed enough oxygen to break down all the lactic acid ✓.

(g) The glucose that Dick used in his race came from his breakfast. Explain how the carbohydrate that Dick ate got into his bloodstream as glucose. **[3]**

> Carbohydrate digested by amylase, in his gut ✓, which is alkaline ✓. The glucose molecules are then absorbed through the gut into the bloodstream ✓.

(h) Once the glucose entered Dicks blood, it was transported to the muscles in his legs. Describe the journey taken by the glucose as it goes from the gut, through the heart and eventually to the leg muscles. **[2]**

> Gut ⟶ heart ⟶ lungs ✓ ⟶ heart ✓ ⟶ leg muscles.

Respiration starts off as aerobic but changes to anaerobic as the supply of oxygen is exceeded by the demand.

If you cannot remember the numbers of atoms, start to balance the equation with the carbon atoms first, then hydrogen and finally oxygen.

Sometimes you are asked to write the word equation rather than the chemical one. If you choose to write down the chemical equation instead, be warned. If you make a mistake you will lose marks on what should have been an easy question.

You can include the word 'energy' in this equation if you wish.

Remember that this is called the 'oxygen debt'.

The two marks are for realising that the blood goes to the lungs and back to the heart.

Sample IGCSE questions

2. A pupil wanted to investigate osmosis in potato tissue. He cut five cylinders from a potato and measured the mass of each. He then placed each block in a different concentration of sucrose solution.

The table shows his results:

Concentration of solution in mol per dm³	Mass of potato cylinder before soaking (in grams)	Mass of potato cylinder after soaking (in grams)	% change in mass
0.0	4.90	5.51	12.40
0.2	4.70	5.10	8.50
0.4	4.80	4.85	1.00
0.6	4.80	4.66	
0.8	5.20	4.81	−7.50

(a) Work out the percentage change in mass for the potato cylinder in the 0.6 mol per dm³ solution. **[2]**

$$4.66 - 4.80 = -0.14 \checkmark \qquad \frac{-0.14 \times 100}{4.80} = 2.9\% \checkmark$$

For percentage change calculations take the starting number away from the final number and multiply by 100.

(b) Plot the results on the grid. **[3]**

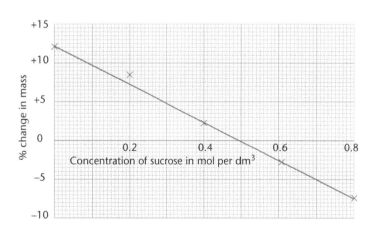

Choose a suitable scale that will use more than half of the graph paper. Make sure that you have a long ruler in order to draw a single straight line.

(c) Finish the graph by drawing the best straight line. **[1]**

(d) Explain what happens to the potato cylinders that were placed in the sucrose solutions with a concentration of more than 0.5 mol per dm³. **[3]**

The potato blocks decreased in mass ✓. This is because their cells are less concentrated than the sucrose solution and so lose water ✓ by osmosis ✓.

Do not say that the sucrose solution moved out of the potato. This is a common mistake.

Exam practice questions

1. Joy has 5 litres of blood. The blood is filtered by her kidneys 250 times every day.

(a) State how many litres of blood are filtered by Joy's kidneys each day. **[2]**

Joy makes a model of her kidney. She puts a cellophane bag of artificial blood into a beaker of distilled warm water.

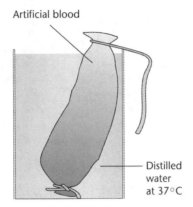

(b) She tests the artificial blood and the distilled water, to see if any of the substances have leaked out of the bag.

	Joy's results		
substance	**found in blood**	**found in water**	**not found in water**
glucose	✓	✓	
salt	✓	✓	
protein	✓		✓
urea	✓	✓	

(i) Explain why Joy kept the distilled water at 37°C. **[1]**

(ii) Name one substance which did not pass out of the bag. **[1]**

(iii) Explain why this substance did not pass out of the bag. **[1]**

(c) Real blood contains red cells and white cells.
Explain the job carried out by each of these types of cell. **[2]**

(d) Joy knows that when kidneys stop working, a person has to use a kidney machine, or have a transplant. Joy's mother carries a kidney donor card but her father does not agree with them.

(i) Suggest two problems faced by a person who has to use a kidney machine. **[2]**

(ii) Explain whether you think that Joy's father should be made to carry a donor card by law. **[3]**

Exam practice questions

2. The diagram shows a cell from a plant.

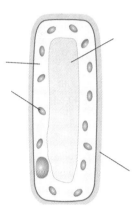

(a) **(i)** Finish the diagram by completing the labels. **[4]**

(ii) Where in a plant does this cell come from? **[1]**

(iii) Name two structures that would not be present if this was an animal cell. **[2]**

(b) This diagram has been drawn using a light microscope. Name one structure found in cells that is too small to be seen with the light microscope. **[1]**

3. The diagram shows an experiment to investigate the uptake of mineral ions into the roots of plants.

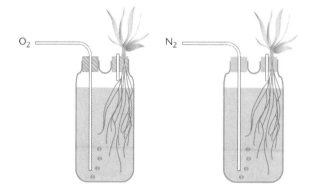

Oxygen or nitrogen gas was bubbled through the water and the uptake of minerals from the solution was measured.

(a) The plant took up more minerals when oxygen was bubbled through the solution. Explain why this is. **[3]**

(b) Waterlogged soil contains little air. Explain why farmers try to make sure their fields are well-drained. **[3]**

Development of the organism and the continuity of life

3.1 Reproduction: In plants

After studying this section you should be able to:

● *define asexual and sexual reproduction*
● *describe asexual reproduction in Bacteria, Fungi and tuber formation in potatoes*
● *describe the structure and function of a dicotyledonous flower*
● *define pollination and state the agents of pollination*
● *describe the process of fertilisation, seed formation and dispersal of seeds*

Like animals, plants give birth to their offspring in a variety of ways. Generally these reproductive procedures can be divided into two major types, asexual and sexual reproduction. Specialities and methods of these two types are described below.

3.1.1 Asexual reproduction

Asexual reproduction is a form of reproduction which does not involve the manufacture and fusion of sex cells or gametes. Asexual reproduction requires only a single parent.

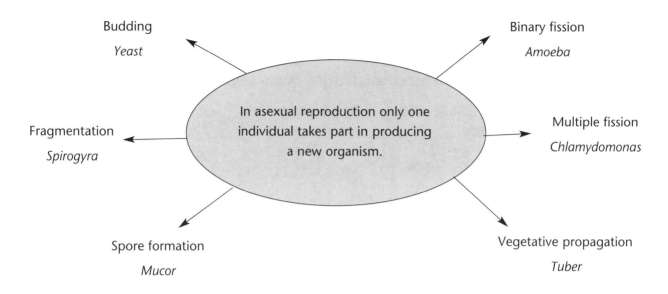

Budding
Yeast

Binary fission
Amoeba

Fragmentation
Spirogyra

In asexual reproduction only one individual takes part in producing a new organism.

Multiple fission
Chlamydomonas

Spore formation
Mucor

Vegetative propagation
Tuber

Main features of asexual reproduction

1. Only one individual is involved.
2. It does not involve production of sex cells.
3. The individuals produced are genetically identical to the parent individual.
4. It shows rapid mode of multiplication.

Bacteria: reproduce by binary fission

The individual cell is fully matured

↓

DNA present in the nucleus divides

↓

Proces of binary fission is shown here

The nucleus divides into two

↓

Cytoplasm divides into two daughter cells

Fungi: reproduce by spore formation

The parent plant produces hundreds of tiny **spores** which can then produce new plants.

• During the growth of a fungus tiny round, bulb like structures called **sporangia** develop at the top of the erect **hyphae**.

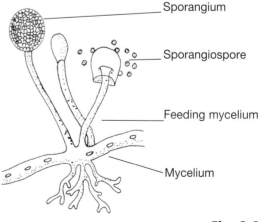

Sporangium

Sporangiospore

Feeding mycelium

Mycelium

Fig. 3.1

- The nucleus divides several times with a bit of cytoplasm and develops into a spore.
- When the sporangium of the plant bursts the spores spread into air.
- When these spores land on favourable substrate they germinate and produce new plants.

Tuber formation in potatoes

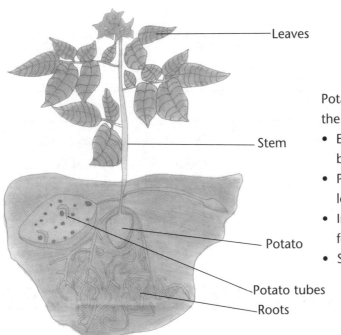

Potatoes are stem tubers. These are swollen up by the depositions of food produced by the plant.
- Each tuber contains stored starch and there are buds on the surface known as eyes.
- Potatoes are cut into small pieces that have at least one eye.
- In suitable condition buds use the stored food to form shoots and roots.
- So each eye of the tuber produces a new plant.

Potatoes: Underground stem

Fig. 3.2

Advantage and disadvantage of asexual reproduction

Advantages	Disadvantages
1. The process is quick.	1. There is little variation.
2. Only one parent is needed.	2. They do not adapt to the changing environment.
3. No gametes are needed.	
4. Without dispersal the plants grow in the same environment as the parent.	3. If the parent has no resistance to a particular disease, none of the offspring will have resistance.
5. It stores large amounts of food that allows rapid growth when conditions are favourable.	4. Lack of dispersal can lead to competition for nutrients, water and light.

3.1.2 Sexual reproduction

> One sex cell fuses with the sex cell of another parent to form a zygote.

The production of a new organism from two parents by making use of their sex cells (or gametes) is called sexual reproduction.

- Humans, fish, frogs, cats, dogs, reproduce sexually.
- Most flowering plants reproduce sexually.

In sexual reproduction two parents are needed to produce new organism.

Advantages and disadvantages of sexual reproduction

Advantages	Disadvantages
1. There is a variation in the offspring. 2. New varieties are produced. 3. In plants seeds are produced and dispersed away from the parent plant, thus reducing competition.	1. Two parents are always needed. 2. Growth of a plant from seed is vegetative propagation.

Structure of a Flower

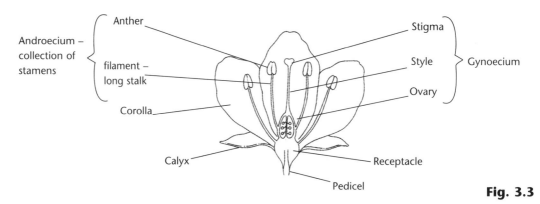

Parts of a typical flower

Fig. 3.3

Function of different parts of a flower

(1) | Stamens make the male gamete which is stored in pollen grains.

(2) | Carpel, the female part of the flower, makes the female gametes. These are stored or are present in ovules.

(3) | Male gametes from the pollen grains travel (get dispersed) and then pollinate and fertilise the female gametes in the ovules.

(4) | The fertilised ovules grow to become the seeds.

Pollination – The transfer of pollen grains from the stamen to the carpel is called pollination.

Pollination is of following two types:

Cross pollination	Self pollination
a. Transfer of pollens from the anther of a plant to stigma of another plant of same species b. Needs agent for pollination i.e., water, insects, birds or man c. Results in healthy and strong offsprings d. Results in production of large number of seeds e. New varieties with useful characters are produced f. Cross pollination is used for producing new kinds of vegetables and fruits g. A plant requires lot of energy and food material to bring about pollination	a. The pollen is transferred to the stigma of the same flower b. Less chances of failure of pollination c. Purity of the race is maintained d. Avoids wastage of pollen grain e. Flowers need not be large and showy f. Continuation of self pollination results in weaker progeny g. New varieties and species of plants are not produced

Differences

Self pollination	Cross pollination
Smaller number of pollen grains are produced	Large number of pollen grains are produced
More chances of successful pollination	Less chances
Less variation	More variation
Less adaptability	More adaptability

Agents of pollination

Air – Maize, Bamboo, Grass
Water – Water plants, *Hydrilla*, Coconut
Insects – Jasmine, Salvia, Garden Pea
Birds – Bombax

Adaptation

Feature	Insect pollinated	Wind pollinated
Petals	Large, colourful, scented	May be absent, or small and inconspicuous
Nectar	Produce nectar to attract insects	Absent, small and green
Stamen	Inside the flower	Long filaments so that the pollens are exposed to wind
Stigma	Small, inside the flower	Large and feathery, hanging outside to catch pollen carried by wind
Pollen	Small amount	Large amount

Growth of pollen tube and fertilisation

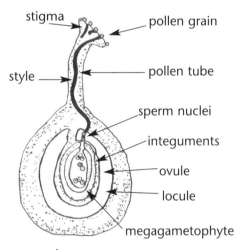

Fig. 3.4

Transfer of pollen grains to gynoecium

Pollen grain of the same species reach the stigma

↓

Pollen tubes are formed, triggered by a sugary solution on the stigma

↓

The pollen tube grows down through the style and reaches the ovule

↓

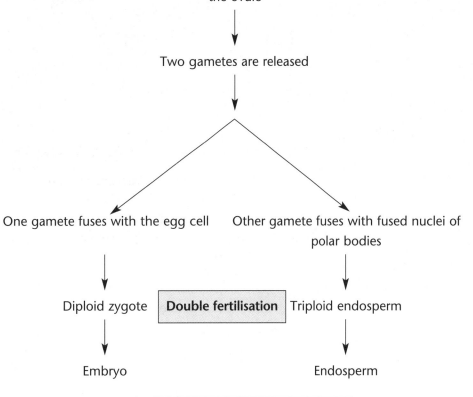

Pollen tube contains two male gametes

↓

This tube pushes its way through the ovary wall and through the micropyle of the ovule

↓

Two gametes are released

One gamete fuses with the egg cell | Other gamete fuses with fused nuclei of polar bodies

Diploid zygote | **Double fertilisation** | Triploid endosperm

Embryo | Endosperm

External fertilisation:

fertilization takes place outside the female body. Frogs and fish show it.

Formation of seed and fruit

- After fertilisation the sepals, petals, stamens, styles and the stigma of the flower wither and fall off.
- The ovary grows rapidly and forms the seed.
- The seed now contains the embryo (tiny root-radicle, shoot-plumule) and the cotyledons.
- The wall of the ovule thickens to form the seed coat or the testa.
- The wall of the ovary grows to form the fruit. It may be fleshy (plum) or dry pod (pea).
- A fruit protects and distributes the seeds.

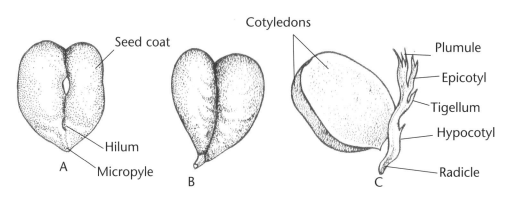

Fig. 3.5

A. Entire seed, B. After removal of seed coat, C. Embryo cotyledons opened.

Structure of seed

Non endospermic seed
- Seed develops from the fertilised ovule and contains an embryonic plant and food store.
- Seed coat or the testa develops from the integuments of the ovule.
- The cotyledons store the food for the baby plant.
- Radicle grows to form the root.
- Plumule grows to form the shoot.

Seed dispersal

Takes place by wind	Takes place by animals
↓	↓
Seeds bear parachute like wing, fine hairs, are very light. e.g. dandelion, sycamore	These seeds belong to succulent fruits or hooked fruits, e.g. bur, black berry

 PROGRESS CHECK

1. Explain briefly the steps involved in the sexual reproduction in plants.
2. Differentiate between self and cross pollination.
3. Name any two characteristics of an insect pollinated flower.
4. What is testa?
5. What is the micropyle?
6. Name the four whorls of a flower.
7. What are the components of stamens?
8. What are the components of a carpel?
9. What do you mean by double fertilisation?
10. What forms the seed?

1. The male organ known as the stamen makes male gametes present in the pollen grains.
   The female part of the flower called the carpel makes the female gametes in the ovules. The male gametes fertilise the female gametes to form the zygote. The zygote grows to form the seeds. These seeds produce new plants.
2. When the pollen grains from the anther of a flower are transferred to the stigma of the same flower, it is called self pollination.
   When the pollen grains from the anther of a flower of one plant is transferred to the stigma of another plant, it is called cross pollination.
3. Colourful petals, nectarines are present.
4. The thick seed coat is called testa.
5. The small opening through which the male gametes enter the ovule.
6. Sepals, petals, stamens, carpel.
7. Filament, anthers.
8. Stigma, style, ovary.
9. One male gamete fuses with the egg to form the zygote, and the other fuses with the two polar nuclei in the middle to give rise to the endosperm.
10. The ovule develops into a seed, zygote forms the embryo, the primary endosperm nucleus gives rise to endosperm and the seed coat.

3.2 Sexual reproduction in humans

After studying this section you should be able to:

● *describe the structure and function of part of the male and female reproductive systems*
● *describe the menstrual cycle*
● *describe sexual intercourse, fertilisation and implantation*
● *describe the development of the foetus*
● *understand the process of birth and antenatal care.*

The primary reproductive organs in the human body are the testes in males and the ovaries in females. Male and female reproductive systems are described below.

3.2.1 Male reproductive system

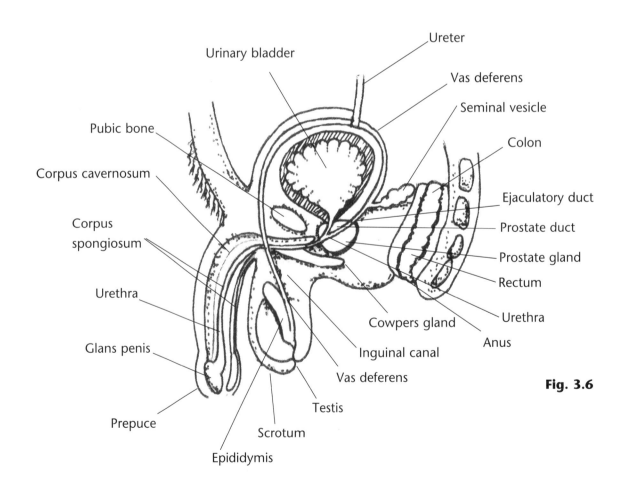

Fig. 3.6

Male reproductive system

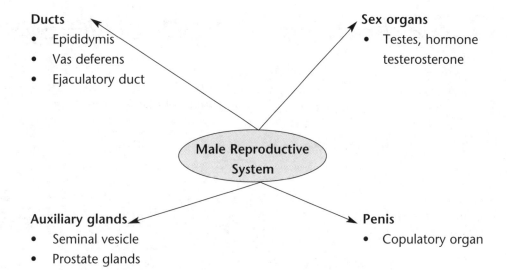

Ducts
- Epididymis
- Vas deferens
- Ejaculatory duct

Sex organs
- Testes, hormone testerosterone

Male Reproductive System

Auxiliary glands
- Seminal vesicle
- Prostate glands
- Cowper's glands

Penis
- Copulatory organ

1. Testes : male gonads that produce sperm
2. Scrotum : a sac that holds the testis outside the body
3. Epididymis : a mass of tubes in which sperms are stored
4. Seminal vesicle : adds fluid and nutrients to sperm to form the semen
5. Sperm duct : muscular tube which links the testis to the urethra to allow the passage of semen containing sperm
6. Prostate gland : adds fluid and nutrients to sperm to form the semen
7. Urethra : to pass semen containing sperm through the penis, also carries urine from the bladder at times
8. Penis : organ to transfer sperm into the vagina

 KEY POINT There is only one opening for urine and sperm to pass out of the body in man.

Puberty: The period when reproductive organs become functional is between ages 13 and 16.

Hormone **testerosterone** is significant in male puberty.

Secondary sexual characteristics:

1. Broadening of shoulders
2. Growth of body hair, chest, face, under arms, pubic area
3. Deepening of voice
4. Increased development of musculature
5. Penis becomes larger
6. Testes starts to produce sperm

3.2.2 Female reproductive system

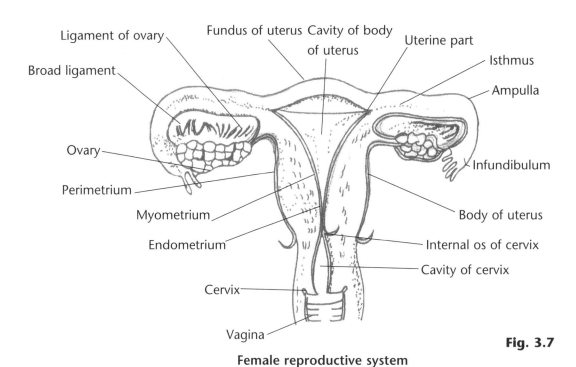

Ligament of ovary
Fundus of uterus Cavity of body of uterus
Uterine part
Isthmus
Ampulla
Broad ligament
Ovary
Infundibulum
Perimetrium
Body of uterus
Myometrium
Internal os of cervix
Endometrium
Cavity of cervix
Cervix
Vagina

Fig. 3.7

Female reproductive system

Functions

1. Ovary: contains follicles in which ova are produced
2. Oviduct: carries the ovum to the uterus. This is the fallopian tube, the site of fertilisation
3. Funnel of oviduct: direct and extends from the ovary to the oviduct
4. Uterus: where the foetus develops
5. Cervix: a ring of muscles that separates the vagina from the uterus
6. Vagina: receives the male penis during intercourse. Sperm is deposited here
7. Urethra: carries urine from the bladder
8. Puberty: period when reproductive organs become functional

Hormones secreted: estrogen and progesterone.

 KEY POINT **Urethra is the opening which passes urine collected from the ureters into the urinary bladder out of the body.**

Secondary sexual characteristics

1. Breasts grow, nipples enlarge.
2. Hair develops under arms and in the pubic area.
3. Hips become wider.

4. Uterus and vagina become larger.
5. Ovaries start to release eggs and menstruation begins.

 1. The release of an ovum (egg) from ovary is called ovulation.
2. Ovulation occurs on 14th day of the next menstrual cycle.

3.2.3 Menstruation

The periodic discharge of blood, mucus and epithelial cells from the lining of the uterus through the vaginal opening is called **menstruation**. It happens every 28 days and lasts for 4–5 days.

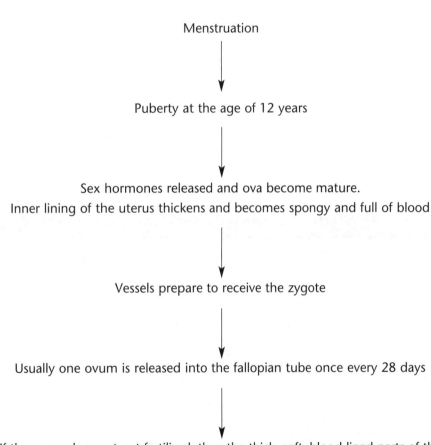

Menstruation

↓

Puberty at the age of 12 years

↓

Sex hormones released and ova become mature.
Inner lining of the uterus thickens and becomes spongy and full of blood

↓

Vessels prepare to receive the zygote

↓

Usually one ovum is released into the fallopian tube once every 28 days

↓

If the ovum does not get fertilised, then the thick, soft, blood-lined parts of the uterus is released out of the vagina in the form of bleeding, called menstruation

↓

After menstruation the ovary and the uterus again get ready to release the ova

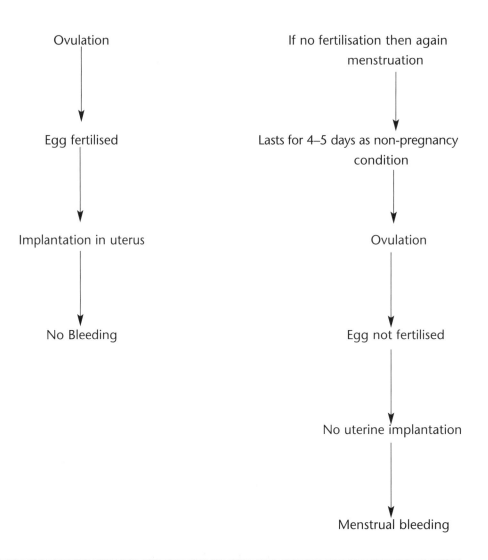

```
Ovulation                        If no fertilisation then again
    |                                      menstruation
    ↓                                           |
Egg fertilised                                  ↓
    |                            Lasts for 4–5 days as non-pregnancy
    ↓                                       condition
Implantation in uterus                          |
    |                                           ↓
    ↓                                       Ovulation
No Bleeding                                     |
                                                ↓
                                         Egg not fertilised
                                                |
                                                ↓
                                         No uterine implantation
                                                |
                                                ↓
                                         Menstrual bleeding
```

Menarche and menopause

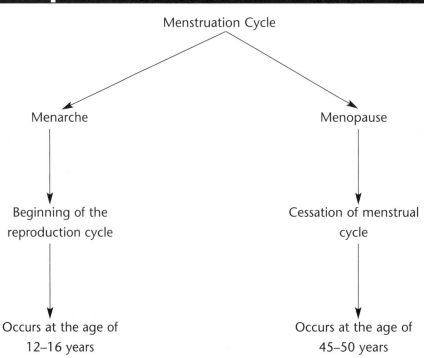

```
                    Menstruation Cycle
                   /                  \
                  ↓                    ↓
             Menarche              Menopause
                |                      |
                ↓                      ↓
         Beginning of the       Cessation of menstrual
        reproduction cycle            cycle
                |                      |
                ↓                      ↓
          Occurs at the age of   Occurs at the age of
            12–16 years            45–50 years
```

Estrogen and progesterone

- Estrogens are responsible for initiating and maintaining the female secondary sexual characteristics and initiating the menstrual cycle.
- Progesterone prepares the reproductive tract for pregnancy.

Sexual Intercourse

This involves insertion of the erect penis into the vagina

1. When blood flows through the penis, it becomes erect.

2. Semen is ejaculated from the penis into the vagina.

3. Muscles in the walls of the sperm ducts help to propel the semen forward.

4. The sperm with their tails swim from the vagina through the cervix, uterus into the fallopian tube.

3.2.4 Fertilisation

Fertilisation:
- **Sperm reaching the fallopian tube has a chance to meet the ovum.**
- **It penetrates the ovum and the zygote is formed.**
- **The zygote rapidly divides by mitosis as it travels down through the fallopian tube forming a small ball of many cells called a blastula.**
- **This ball of cells becomes embedded or implanted in the mucosa of the uterus.**

- **Ovum is produced only every 28th day.**
- **Ovum cannot be fertilised after 48 hours of ovulation.**
- **Sperms live for only 48 hours.**
- **So intercourse around the period of ovulation is important for fertilisation.**

Development of the foetus:

- In humans, the egg is without reserve nutrients.

- The embryo gets nutrients and oxygen from the mother until birth.

- The embryo develops three embryonic membranes that surround it.

Amniotic sac – membrane formed from cell of the embryo, which contains amniotic fluid, encloses the developing foetus and prevents entry of bacteria.

Amniotic fluid – supports the foetus, protecting it from physical damage. It absorbs excretory materials (urine) released by the foetus.

After implantation an organic connection is established between the extra embryonic membranes of the embryo and the uterine wall of the mother known as placenta.

 KEY POINT   **Placenta is connected with the embryo through the umbilical cord.**

The functions of the placenta are:
1. receiving dissolved food substance from the mother's blood
2. receiving oxygen from the mother's blood
3. excreting CO_2 and nitrogenous waste
4. serving as an important but temporary endocrine gland.

Ante-natal care

- Before the birth or during pregnancy all the dietary requirements of the baby/foetus are obtained from the mother through the placenta.

- So a mother's diet needs to be balanced so that the foetus receives all the nutrients it needs for its growth and development.

Balanced diet includes:

- protein for growth

- calcium for development of the skeleton

- iron for RBC development of the skeleton

- vitamin C for good bones and skin

- carbohydrates and fats for energy

- vitamins and minerals to prevent any deficiency

But, other than a balanced diet, drugs, medicines, alcohol, cigarette smoke and viruses can pass across the placenta, risking the health of the developing foetus.

Advantages of breast feeding

1. Breast milk contains antibodies providing immunity to the baby.

2. Breast milk is a balanced diet for the baby.

3. No chemicals are present which make it free from allergies.

4. It does not need sterilisation and it is totally safe for the child.

5. Good for the mother too as it triggers a reduction in the size of the mother's uterus.

Process of birth

Labour – triggered by hormone oxytocin

↓

Muscular walls of the uterus start to contract

↓

The pressure breaks the amniotic sac

↓

Contractions become more frequent pushing the baby down towards the cervix

↓

Cervix becomes dilated to allow the baby to pass

↓

The vagina too stretches for the passage of the baby

↓

The baby is still attached to the placenta by the umbilical cord

↓

Placenta breaks away from the uterine wall and passes out

↓

Umbilical cord is cut and tied

PROGRESS CHECK

1. Why are the scrotal sacs placed outside the body of man?
2. State the functions of the following:
   a. Testorosterone
   b. Oviduct
   c. Seminal vesicle
   d. Penis
3. What is semen? Where is it produced and stored?
4. What are the secondary sexual characteristics of a male?
5. What is ovulation? When does it occur?
6. What happens to the ovum if it is not fertilised?
7. What is the placenta? What is its main function?
8. Explain the following terms:
   a. Gestation period
   b. Menstrual cycle
   c. Menarche
   d. Pregnancy
   e. Menopause
9. What is intercourse?
10. How does fertilisation take place?

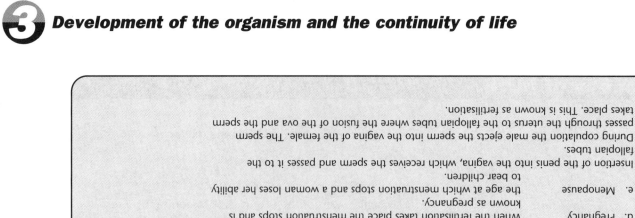

PROGRESS CHECK

1. Scrotal sacs are placed outside the body as the sperms mature at a temperature slightly lower than the body temperature.
2. a. Testosterone — this hormone causes growth and maturation of the secondary sexual characteristics in males.
   b. Oviduct — the ovum is fertilised here.
   c. Seminal vesicles — secretes fluid which forms much of the semen.
   d. Penis — copulatory organ which deposits semen into vagina of the female.
3. Semen is a fluid containing sperm. They are stored in the epididymis.
4. Broadening of shoulders, growth of body hair, deepening of voice, development of musculature.
5. The process of release of the ripe egg from the ovary is called ovulation. It occurs every 14th day before the next menstrual cycle.
6. It dies 48 hours after secretion, if not fertilised.
7. The membranous connection between the foetus and the mother. The main function is to supply food, blood and oxygen to the foetus and remove the waste products.
8. a. Gestation period — the development of the foetus for 9 months in the mother's uterus.
   b. Menstrual cycle — the breakdown and removal of the inner thick and soft lining of the uterus along with its blood vessels in the form of vaginal bleeding.
   c. Menarche — the beginning of menstruation at puberty.
   d. Pregnancy — When the fertilisation takes place the menstruation stops and is known as pregnancy.
   e. Menopause — the age at which menstruation stops and a woman loses her ability to bear children.
9. Insertion of the penis into the vagina, which receives the sperm and passes it to the fallopian tubes.
10. During copulation the male ejects the sperm into the vagina of the female. The sperm passes through the uterus to the fallopian tubes where the fusion of the ova and the sperm takes place. This is known as fertilisation.

3.2.5 Methods of birth control

In order to reduce the population pressure different birth control methods are practised throughout the world. They are categorised into following four major types:

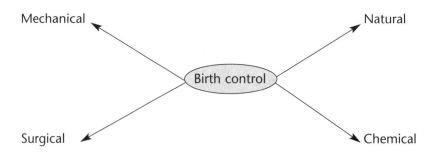

Each of these methods are summarised here.

Mechanical methods

- Use of condom
- A rubber sheath placed to stop sperm entering the vagina
- Also prevents veneral diseases spreading

- Femidom
- A plastic sheath placed inside the vagina
- Prevents entry of sperm
- Prevents sexually transmitted diseases

- Diaphragm
- Dome shaped rubber barrier fitted in the cervix by a doctor
- Prevents the entry of sperm into the cervix

- IUD/Intrauterine device
- Plastic-coated copper coil is surgically inserted into the wall of the uterus
- Prevents implantation of blastula

Natural methods

- Withdrawl
- Withdrawl of penis before ejaculation
- Not very reliable

- Abstinence
- No sexual intercourse
- Most reliable

- Rhythm method
- Intercourse is avoided at the ovulation period
- Cannot be exactly predicted

Chemical methods

- Contraception pill
- Contains progesterone and oestrogen which prevent ovulation
- Progesterone only prevents implantation of blastula

- Spermicidal
- Kills sperm in the vagina
- Should only be used with condom/diaphragm

Surgical methods

- Vasectomy
- Sperm ducts are tied or cut
- So no sperm leaves the testes
- Not normaly reversible but extremely reliable

- Laparotomy/tubectomy
- Oviducts are tied or cut
- No eggs/ova can pass down

Artificial insemination

Method by which a woman can have a baby when the male partner is infertile.

Sperm from a donor (stored in a sperm bank)

Inserted into the female uterus around the time of ovulation

> Argument: the child has the right to know who the real father is.
> But many sperm donors like to remain anonymous.

Use of hormones in fertility drugs

Following hormones are used to increase the chance of pregnancy:

FSH – Follicle stimulating hormone

LH – Luteinizing hormone

> These hormones lead to multiple releases of ova

In-vitro fertilisation

- If the oviducts are blocked the doctor collects the ova produced by FSH and LH.
- The ova are fertilised in a petridish using the male partner's sperm.
- The early embryo produced is then inserted into the uterus to achieve pregnancy.

Sexually transmitted diseases

These diseases are passed on during unprotected sexual intercourse.

Gonorrhoea:

- Caused by diplococcus *Neisseria gonorrhoea*
- Transmitted by sexual act with more than one partner

  Symptoms in males

  - sores on penis
  - urethra becomes inflamed and pus is discharged
  - pain/burning sensation while urinating
  - may spread to ovary and female reproductive organs

Symptoms in females

- sometimes discharge of pus from vagina
- often with no symptoms

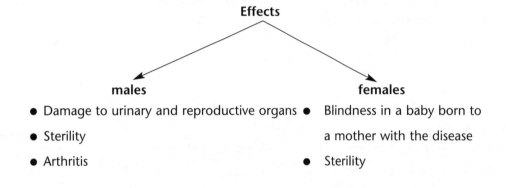

Effects

males
- Damage to urinary and reproductive organs
- Sterility
- Arthritis

females
- Blindness in a baby born to a mother with the disease
- Sterility

HIV (Human Immunodeficiency Virus) – A virus which destroys the immune system. It may result in AIDS (Acquired Immune Deficiency Syndrome)

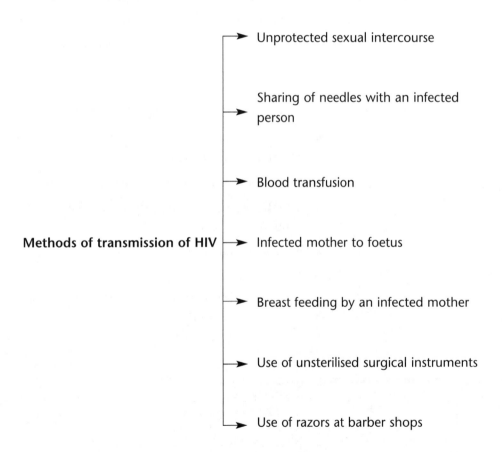

Methods of transmission of HIV
- Unprotected sexual intercourse
- Sharing of needles with an infected person
- Blood transfusion
- Infected mother to foetus
- Breast feeding by an infected mother
- Use of unsterilised surgical instruments
- Use of razors at barber shops

Ways to prevent the spread of HIV

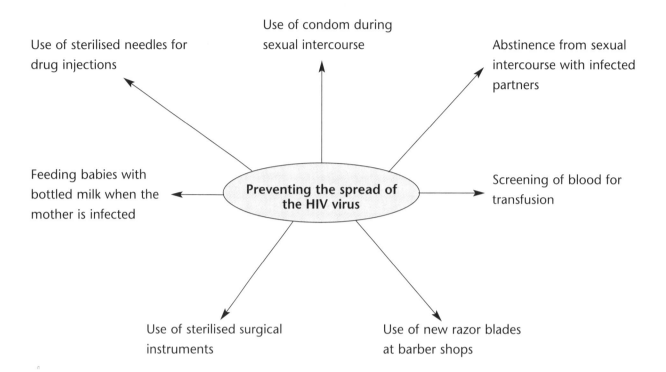

Use of condom during sexual intercourse

Use of sterilised needles for drug injections

Abstinence from sexual intercourse with infected partners

Feeding babies with bottled milk when the mother is infected

Preventing the spread of the HIV virus

Screening of blood for transfusion

Use of sterilised surgical instruments

Use of new razor blades at barber shops

How HIV affects the immune system

- Lymphocytes in the blood produce antibodies which attack the antigens present in the invading bacteria.

- The HIV virus attaches to these lymphocytes and destroys them.

- Since the protecting lymphocytes are destroyed the immune system becomes very weak.

- So the AIDS sufferer has no protection against disease.

Most common infections due to AIDS are:

- Tuberculosis

- Pneumonia

1. Name three methods used for birth control
2. What is the surgical method of birth control which is carried out in
   a. males   b. females
3. What are sexually transmitted diseases.
4. Name two devices used in the barrier method of birth control.
5. How can HIV spread be prevented?
6. How does HIV effect the immune system?

 PROGRESS CHECK

1. Mechanical, chemical, surgical.
2. a. Vasectomy, b. Tubectomy
3. Diseases which are transmitted due to sexual contact.
4. Condoms, diaphragm.
5. Use of condoms, screening of blood before transfusion, use fresh needles for injections.
6. It destroys lymphocytes and reduces immunity.

3.3 Growth and development

After studying this section you should be able to:
- define growth and development
- explain development with the help of an example
- describe the environmental factors affecting germination.

Growth: Growth is the increase in the number of cells due to mitotic division. It is controlled by hormones in animals and auxins in plants.

 Growth is measured in dry mass and wet mass.

Dry mass: the value of the dry mass would be obtained by drying out the moisture from the organism (so it has to be killed).
- There is always a minor drop in dry mass as a seed germinates from the second day.
- Dry mass drops at the end of the growth period due to the loss of seeds and fruits or leaves.

Wet mass: mass, height, surface area (leaves), volume, number of leaves, body length, etc. can be used to measure growth.
- But all these are not reliable; some are tall, others are short, some plants have large leaves others have small ones.
- Mass may be the storage of fat which is not actual growth.

Development
- Increase in complexity of an organism.
- Multicellular organisms have got many different functions to perform, so the cells have to be assigned different jobs to do.
- For the special jobs to perform, they need to change and adapt themselves.

Environmental factors that affect germination

Seed is a living structure, protected and adapted to survive till it gets all the condition necessary for germination.

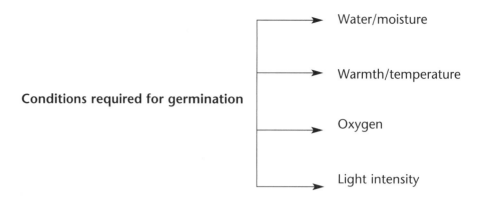

Conditions required for germination

→ Water/moisture

→ Warmth/temperature

→ Oxygen

→ Light intensity

Water: needed, to activate enzymes for converting soluble food stores in the cotyledons down to soluble food which can be used for growth by the baby plant.

Warmth/temperature: enzymes present in the seed get activated and work best at optimum temperature (20–40° C) which triggers growth in the baby plant.

Oxygen: needed for respiration as soon as the growth process begins. It is required for energy to mobilise the chemical changes.

Light intensity: high or very low light intensity does not allow the enzymes to function normally.

 PROGRESS CHECK

1. What do you understand by growth?
2. What is development?
3. State the environmental factors which effect germination.
4. Why does a seed require water for germination?

1. Growth is the increase in the number of cells.
2. Increase in the complexity and the number of cells in an organism.
3. Moisture, temperature, oxygen, light intensity.
4. The food is present in insoluble form and to make it available to the baby plant it has to be dissolved.

3.4 Inheritance

After studying this section you should be able to:

- *explain how sex is determined*
- *understand monohybrid inheritance*
- *explain how some diseases are inherited*
- *understand the gene*
- *understand cloning, selective breeding and genetic engineering*
- *define terms of importance*
- *describe the inheritance of sex in humans*
- *describe mitosis and meiosis*

Chromosomes: Humans have 46 chromosomes in pairs.

Each chromosome is made up of large number of genes.

Genes are the codes which form different proteins.

Proteins give us our distinct characteristics.

Gene: a section of DNA, which codes for the protein controlling a specific characteristic of the organism.

Sex determination

Humans have 23 pairs of **chromosomes**. The chromosomes of one of these pairs are called the sex chromosomes because they carry the genes that determine the sex of the person.

- **Females have two X chromosomes and are XX.**

- **Males have one X and one Y chromosome and are XY.**

> **KEY POINT**
> There are two kinds of sex chromosomes. One is called X and one is called Y.

This means that females produce ova that contain single X chromosomes and males produce sperm, half of which contain a Y chromosome and half of which contain an X chromosome.

Boys inherit an X chromosome from their mother and a Y chromosome from their father.

Girls inherit an X chromosome from their mother and an X chromosome from their father.

Fig. 3.8

	X	Y
X	XX	XY
X	XX	XY

Monohybrid inheritance

Gregor Mendel was an Augustinian monk who did experiments with pea plants. He studied monohybrid inheritance in pea plants.

Monohybrid inheritance

This involves the study of how a single gene is passed on from parents to offspring.

A cross between heterozygous tall pea plants:

The tall variety is dominant.

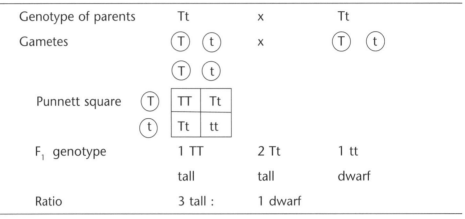

Genotype of parents	Tt	x	Tt
Gametes	T t	x	T t
	T t		
Punnett square	T | TT | Tt		
	t | Tt | tt		
F$_1$ genotype	1 TT	2 Tt	1 tt
	tall	tall	dwarf
Ratio	3 tall :	1 dwarf	

The cross between a heterozygous tall pea plant and a dwarf pea plant.

Phenotype	tall		dwarf
Genotype of parents	Tt	x	tt
Gametes	T t	x	t t
	t t		
Punnett square	T | Tt | Tt		
	t | tt | tt		
F$_1$ genotype	2 Tt,	2 tt	
	2 tall	2 dwarf	
Ratio	1 tall :	1 dwarf	

- **Law of segregation** – the alleles of a gene separate into different gametes.
- **Law of independent assortment** – any male gamete can fertilise any female gamete.

Mendel could not back up his ideas as the technology of modern microscopes had not yet been discovered. It was many years before the science of modern genetics was born.

We now know that we inherit 23 chromosomes from mother and 23 chromosomes from father.

KEY POINT   This means that we each get two sets of instructions.

A good example to explain this is tongue rolling. The two alleles for tongue rolling are:

● YES – you can roll your tongue

● NO – you cannot roll your tongue

This means that the possible combinations we can inherit are:

Allele – A gene controlling a character may have two or sometimes more alternative forms. Each form of a gene is called an allele.

Allele from mother	Allele from father	What the baby gets
YES	YES	YES YES
YES	NO	YES NO
NO	YES	YES NO
NO	NO	NO NO

If the alleles agree with each other there is no problem, but sometimes the alleles disagree about tongue rolling. When this happens, tongue rolling is always **dominant** and non-tongue rolling is always **recessive**.

> This means that only people with NO, NO will *not* be able to roll their tongue.

Instead of using YES and NO we use a capital **T** for tongue rolling and a lower case **t** for non-tongue rolling.

> **KEY POINT**
>
> Words you need to know:
> homozygous – both alleles agree
> heterozygous – both alleles disagree
> genotype – which type of alleles make up the gene
> phenotype – how the gene expresses itself

Some examples

Mother and father are both **homozygous**. Father's **phenotype** is a tongue roller. Mother's phenotype is a non-tongue roller.

> All the children are hetrozygous tongue rollers.

	Mother	
	t	t
Father T	Tt	Tt
Father T	Tt	Tt

All are tongue rollers

In this example, both the parents are **heterozygous** and have the phenotype of a tongue roller.

> Three out of four can roll their tongues. One out of four cannot roll their tongues. This is a 3:1 ratio.

	Mother	
	T	t
Father T	Tt	Tt
Father t	Tt	tt

Cannot roll tongue

Dominant – the allele which dominates the other alternative form or expresses itself in F1 hybrid is called dominant.

Recessive – the allele which fails to express in F1 hybrids or whose expression is masked by dominant gene.

Haploid	– a cell which contains only one chromosome from each homozygous pair, i.e. only one set of chromosomes.
Diploid	– an individual or cell which contains paired chromosomes is diploid.
Genotype	– genetic make up of an organism.
Phenotype	– phenotype is the expression or appearance of a character of an organism.
Homozygous	– an organism whose genotype for a particular character contains identical alleles.
Heterozygous	– an organism whose genotype for a particular character contains two different alleles.

Codominance

The term describes a pair of alleles, neither of which is dominant over the other. This means both the alleles have the ability to affect the phenotype when they are present together in the genotype

Inheritance of A, B, AB and O blood groups

These blood groups give an example of codominance. Instead of 2 alleles present in this case there are 3 alleles, i.e. — I^A I^B and I^O.

Combination of these can result in four phenotypes A, B, AB, O

The alleles are responsible for producing antigens responsible for immunity.

e.g., Two parents have blood groups A and B.

The father $I^A I^O$ and mother is $I^B I^O$

Phenotype of parents	blood group A			blood group B	
Genotype	$I^A I^O$			$I^B I^O$	
Gametes	I^A I^O		x	I^B I^O	

Punnett square

	I^A	I^O
I^B	$I^A I^B$	$I^O I^B$
I^O	$I^A I^O$	$I^O I^O$

F$_1$ genotypes	$I^A I^O$	$I^B I^O$	$I^A I^B$	$I^O I^O$
	A	B	AB	O
Ratio	1 :	1 :	1 :	1

The gene

DNA is the chemical language of life. Unlike English which has 26 letters, the language of DNA has 4 chemical 'letters'. These 'letters' are:

- **A**denine
- **T**hymine
- **G**uanine
- **C**ytosine.

Tens of thousands of these bases are arranged along the DNA and spell out the instructions for making proteins.

... ATTGCACTGACTGCATAAGTGTCAACACTCGAG ...

To interpret this language we need to know that three bases are the code for one amino acid... and amino acids join together to make protein.

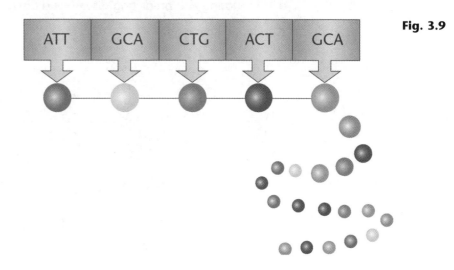

Fig. 3.9

A gene is all the bases on the DNA that code for one protein.

DNA: the double helix

Complementary base pairs

- DNA is the hereditary material.
- The helical structure was enumerated by **Watson** and **Crick**.

DNA actually consists of two strands and is coiled into a double helix. The strands are linked together by a series of paired bases.

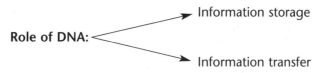

Role of DNA: → Information storage
→ Information transfer

A always pairs with T.
G always pairs with C.

A-T
T-A
T-A
G-C

Fig. 3.10

Scientists around the world have finally completed the decoding of all the bases in the human DNA. This means we now have a genetic map of all the human genes. This is an amazing and historical achievement and will enable massive advances in medical care and genetic engineering.

This is called the Human Genome Project.

Applications

- Diagnosing and predicting disease and disease susceptibility
- Disease intervention

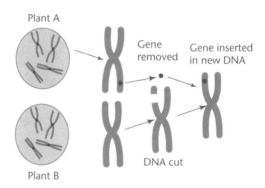

Plant A

Plant B

Gene removed

Gene inserted in new DNA

DNA cut

Fig. 3.11

PROGRESS CHECK

1. Where do boys inherit their Y chromosome from?
2. Explain Mendel's 'Law of Segregation'.
3. State the genotype of a non-tongue roller.
4. If dad is a homozygous tongue roller and mum is a homozygous non-tongue roller, what proportion of their children will be homozygous?
5. If mother and father are heterozygous, what proportion of their children will be non-tongue rollers?
6. State why there are no 'carriers' for the disease Huntington's chorea.
7. State why both mother and father have to be carriers, to produce a child with cystic fibrosis.
8. A Down's syndrome child has 47 chromosomes. State why the ovum with 22 chromosomes is rarely fertilised.
9. State how many bases code for one amino acid.
10. State the name of the section of DNA that codes for one protein.
11. State three different ways of performing micropropagation.
12. Explain how selective breeding could be used to increase a cattle herd's milk yield.
13. How many pairs of chromosomes are present in human beings?
14. What is the difference between the cells formed after mitosis and meiosis?
15. What are the characteristic features of Huntington's chorea ?
16. Which type of reproduction requires only one parent? Why?
17. What is the role of DNA?

1. Father; 2. Alleles of a gene separate into different gametes; 3. tt; 4. None; 5. 1 in 4 (3:1); 6. It is a dominant gene and anyone with the gene will have the disease; 7. It is recessive and the child must inherit a recessive allele from both parents; 8. One chromosome is missing making it infertile; 9. Three; 10. Gene; 11. Tissue culture, embryo transplants, nuclear transplants; 12. Breed from high yield cows and bulls who produced high yield milk. 13. 23 pairs 14. Mitosis: the daughter cells would have the same number of chromosomes as the parent. Meiosis: the daughter cell would have half the number of chromosomes. 15. Progressive mental and physical deterioration. 16. Asexual reproduction which uses only mitotic cell division. 17. It stores information and transfers it wherever necessary.

3.5 Variation

LEARNING SUMMARY

After studying this section you should be able to:

- *explain the causes of variation*
- *understand the role of sexual and asexual reproduction in variation*
- *understand what a mutation is*
- *explain the causes of mutation*
- *explain continuous and discontinuous variation*
- *explain variation and the role of competition in natural selection.*

What is variation

Variation is the differences found within a population of organisms.

It is of two types:

Variation

Continuous

Discontinuous

- different characteristics within a population
- height, body, mass, intelligence

- distinct features
- blood group, tongue roll, ear lobe

Causes of variation

Children born from the same parents all look slightly different. We call these differences 'variation'

- **inherited or genetic** – some variation is inherited from our parents.

- **environmental** – some variation is a result of our environment.

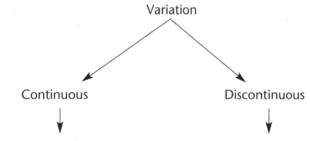

Remember: variation can arise in two ways.

Examples of different kinds of variation	
Inherited	**Environmental**
eye colour	sun tan
blood group	scar tissue
finger prints	tattoos
hair colour	hair length
height and weight	
These can be a combination of both inherited and environmental causes.	

Development of the organism and the continuity of life

A good way to think of it, is that the genes provide a height and weight range into which we will fit, and how much we eat determines where in that range we will be.

Scientists have argued for many years whether 'nature' or 'nurture' (inheritance or environment), is responsible for intelligence.

Fig. 3.12

A scientist called **Francis Galton** thought that intelligence was inherited and that the environment had nothing to do with it. The argument can be resolved by studying identical twins that have been separated at birth.

Genetically, both twins are the same. Therefore any differences between them must be due to the environment. Tests on identical twins tell us that intelligence is a mixture of both our genes and the environment.

How sexual reproduction leads to variation

Sexual reproduction involves the joining together of male and female gametes.

The gametes contain chromosomes on which are found genes. Genes are the instructions that make an organism.

Both the mother and the father like all other humans have 46 (23 pairs) of chromosomes in most of the cells of their bodies. This is called the **diploid** number.

This type of cell division is called meiosis.

Males produce sperms that contain 23 chromosomes. One from each pair.

Females produce ova that contain 23 chromosomes. One from each pair. This is called the **haploid** number.

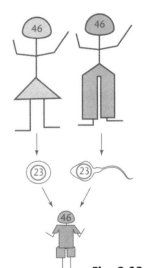

When a sperm fertilises an ovum, the number returns to 46 (23 pairs).

If this did not happen, the number of chromosomes would double with each generation.

Fig. 3.13

Because the baby can receive any one of the 23 pairs from its mother and any one of the 23 pairs from its father, the number of possible gene combinations is enormous. This new mixture of genetic information produces a great deal of variation in the offspring.

How asexual reproduction leads to clones

> This type of cell division is called mitosis.

Asexual reproduction is when cells divide to make identical copies of themselves. The number of chromosomes stays the same. Plants and animals do this when they grow.

Some plants grow so much that they produce smaller plants. This is called asexual reproduction, as there is no sex involved.

Fig. 3.14

Only one individual is needed for asexual reproduction.

The 'baby' plants are genetically identical to their parents. They are called **clones**. When you go into a shop and buy some strawberries, all the strawberries are genetically identical. You are eating strawberry clones.

Mutation – a source of variation

Mutations are changes to the base pair sequence of genetic material (either DNA or RNA). Mutations can be caused by copying errors in the genetic material during cell division and by exposure to ultraviolet or ionising radiation, chemical mutagens, or viruses, or it can occur deliberately under cellular control during processes such as meiosis.

Mutation is of the following two types that can lead to different disorders in the human body.

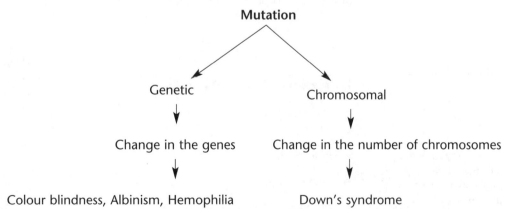

A mutation is a random change to the structure of DNA. DNA has a language just like English, but whereas English has 26 letters, DNA has just 4 chemical 'letters'. These four 'letters' are called bases.

A mutation happens when one of these chemical 'letters' is changed. Mutation is most unlikely to benefit the organism.

Think what would happen if you made random changes to a few of the letters on this page. It is most likely to produce gibberish and very unlikely to make any sense at all.

- If a mutation occurs in a gamete, the offspring may develop abnormally and could pass the mutation onto their own offspring.

- If a mutation occurs in a body cell, it could start to multiply out of control – this is **cancer**.

> On very rare occasions, however, a single random mutation can make a major change to what the gene is saying.

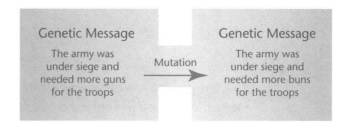

Fig. 3.15

On the rare occasions when a beneficial mutation occurs, natural selection ensures that it will increase in the population.

Down's syndrome

Down's syndrome occurs when the ovum that is fertilised has an extra chromosome. This happens because at meiosis, the chromosomes do not divide properly. One ovum gets 22 and is infertile. The other gets 24. This extra set of genetic instructions usually results in some degree of mental and physical disability.

> The baby will have 47 chromosomes instead of the usual number of 46.

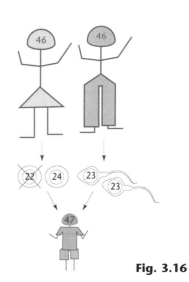

Fig. 3.16

Causes of mutations:

- radiation
- UV in sunlight
- X-Rays
- chemical mutagens – as found in cigarettes

> Anything that changes or damages the genes on the DNA can cause a mutation.

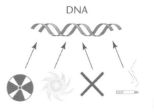

DNA

Fig. 3.17

Different causes of mutation

Effect of radiation

High energy radiation from a radioactive material or from X-rays is absorbed by the atoms in water molecules surrounding the DNA. The energy is transferred to the electrons which then fly from the atom. Left behind is a **free radical**, which is a highly dangerous and reactive molecule that attacks the DNA molecule and alters it in many ways. Radiation can also cause double strand breaks in the DNA molecule, by which the cell's repair mechanisms cannot put right.

Radiation excites electrons to a higher energy level. Electrons of DNA molecules get excited by absorbing UV light. Two nucleotide bases in DNA cytosine and thymine – are most vulnerable to excitation that can change base pairing properties.

Effect of UV rays of the Sun

Sunlight contains ultraviolet radiation (the component that causes sun tan) which, when absorbed by the DNA forms a cross link between certain adjacent bases. In most cases the cells can repair this damage, but unrepaired **dimers** of this sort cause the replicating system to skip over the mistake leaving a gap, which is supposed to be filled in later.

Unprotected exposure to UV radiation by the human skin can cause serious damage and may lead to skin cancer and extensive skin tumors.

Chemical Mutagens

Chemical Mutagens change the sequence of bases in DNA by a number of ways:

- they mimic the correct nucleotide bases in a DNA molecule, but fail to base pair correctly during DNA replication
- they remove parts of the nucleotide (such as the amino group on adenine), again causing improper base pairing during DNA replication
- they add hydrocarbon groups to various nucleotides, also causing incorrect base pairing during DNA replication.

Sickle cell anaemia and its relation to malaria

- Sickle cell anaemia is caused by a mutation in the blood pigment haemoglobin.
- When this faulty hemoglobin is formed it becomes sickle shaped and is incapable of carrying oxygen.
- Since they change their shape they get stuck in the capillaries preventing blood flow.

Malaria is a life threatening disease caused by protozoa which invades red blood cells.

- A heterozygous person having the gene for sickle cell anaemia ($H^N H^n$) is protected for malaria, because the protozoa is unable to invade the sickle cells.

- A person homozygous for sickle cell ($H^n H^n$) also has protection.

- A person with normal haemoglobin ($H^N H^N$) is at high risk of transmitting malaria because they are not protected by the sickle cell.

PROGRESS CHECK

1. Which of the following examples of variation is inherited?
    sun tan   tattoo   eye colour   scar tissue
2. Who was the scientist who thought intelligence was inherited?
3. Which type of reproduction produces variation in the offspring?
4. Name one other source of variation.
5. List four things that can cause mutations.
6. Why do mother and father have 46 chromosomes, but produce sperm and ova with only 23?
7. What type of cell division leads to the production of clones?
8. What are the differences between heritable and environmental variations?
9. What are genes and where are these located?
10. What do you mean by variations? Give two examples.
11. What is mutation?

1. Eye colour;   2. Francis Galton;   3. Sexual reproduction;   4. Mutation;   5. Radiation, UV light, X-Rays, chemical mutagens – as found in cigarettes;   6. So that after fertilisation, the number in the baby returns to 46;   7. Mitosis.   8. Heritable variations are differences in the genetic compositions of individuals. Environmental variations are closely related forms caused by food, temperature, moisture, light, altitude, etc. 9. Genes are the hereditary units which are situated on the chromosomes. 10. The differences in the characters (or traits) among the individuals of a species is called variation.
Human height, hair.
11. Mutation is the sudden change in the genetic make up of an organism.

Selection

Definition of selection

Selection is the process by which those organisms which appear physically, physiologically and behaviourally better adapted to the environment survive and reproduce; those organisms not so well adapted either fail to reproduce or die.

Selection is of two types: **natural** and **artificial selection**.

Natural selection is done by the organisms themselves. But artificial selection is used by humans to produce varieties of animals and plants that have an increased economic importance.

- This process is also known as hybridisation where a new variety is produced by crossing between two varieties which are selected.

e.g.,   **High yield variety**

Vs.

Disease resistant variety

When these two varieties are crossed a new variety with high yield and disease resistance is produced.

3.6 Genetic engineering

LEARNING SUMMARY

After studying this section you should be able to:

- understand the structure of DNA (Deoxyribonucleic Acid)
- understand how DNA makes proteins
- understand how the genes that cause genetic diseases can be found
- understand how genetic engineering works.

This means the DNA of a frog would be understood by the DNA of a daffodil.

KEY POINT

Genetic engineering is a process by which a gene is taken from a chromosome of one species and put into the chromosome of another species.

All living organisms use the same language of DNA. The four letters A, G, C and T are the same in all living things. Thus a gene from one organism can be removed and placed in a totally different organism where it will continue to carry out its function.

Structure of DNA

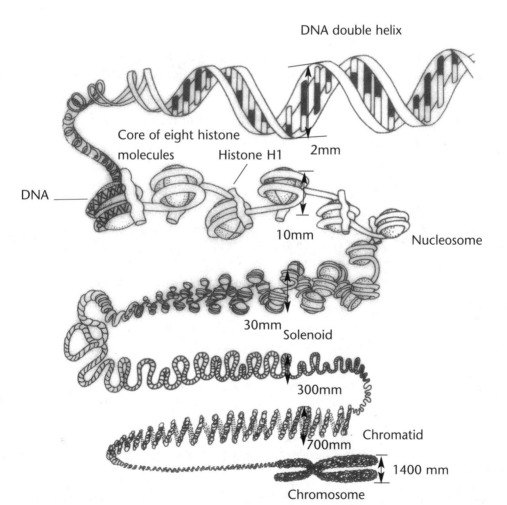

Fig. 3.18

Structure of DNA

DNA – key facts

- The language of DNA is universal and understood by all living organisms.
- DNA has two jobs, code for information and copying itself.
- The language has four letters. They are the bases **A**, **T**, **C** and **G**.
- Bases go together in pairs, **A** with **T** and **C** with **G**. This makes DNA a double strand.
- The sequence of bases codes for information, just like the sequence of letters in English.
- Only one strand carries the message. This is called the 'sense' strand.
- The bases are held together by a ribose sugar attached to a phosphate molecule.
- DNA copies itself just before the cell divides. This ensures each new cell has an exact copy.
- To copy itself, DNA 'unzips' between the bases. Because **A** only pairs with **T** and **C** with **G**, a new copy is quickly made.

Protein synthesis

DNA is much too precious to be allowed outside the cell. It is kept safe inside the nucleus. Instructions are sent out from the nucleus into the cell. These instructions are made from **mRNA**. The 'm' stands for 'messenger' because it carries a message.

> **KEY POINT**
>
> **Differences between DNA and mRNA:**
> - **RNA has a four-letter code but T is replaced by U.**
> - **DNA has two strands but mRNA has only one.**
> - **The mRNA is a copy of a single gene.**

When an architect designs a building he does not give his original plans to the builder. He gives the builder a copy and keeps his original plans safe and out of harm's way.

GENE (Usually contains several hundred bases)

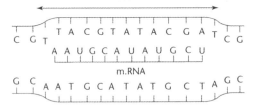

Fig. 3.19

Remember: one gene = one instruction = makes one protein.

Once the mRNA has left the nucleus, it lines itself up on a structure called a **ribosome**.

The ribosome is like a 'tape head' in a video player. It reads the message.

Remember: proteins are made from up to twenty different amino acids. This means that there must be at least twenty different words.

The message consists of words, all of which have three 'letters' or 'bases'. Each word codes for a different amino acid. Unlike the English language, there are no spaces between the words.

The protein is put together by another kind of RNA called **tRNA**. The 't' stands for 'transfer', because it transfers amino acids to the ribosome. There is a different kind of tRNA for each different amino acid. The tRNA attaches to its amino acid and when the correct three letter sequence reaches the ribosome, the tRNA connects the amino acids to make the protein.

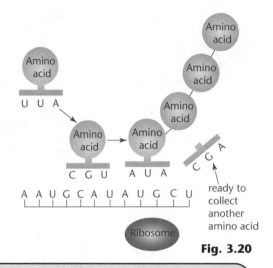

Fig. 3.20

PROGRESS CHECK

1. State which base pairs with C and which base pairs with T.
2. State how many bases code for one amino acid.
3. DNA does not leave the nucleus. State how it gets the instructions on how to make proteins inside the cell.
4. State which type of RNA carries the amino acid to the ribosome.
5. If a section of DNA has the sequence CGA, state the sequence on the mRNA and the sequence on the tRNA.
6. State two differences between DNA and RNA.
7. State the two functions of DNA.
8. DNA has two strands. Explain why the 'message' is carried by only one of the strands.

1. G and A;   2. Three;   3. Makes an mRNA copy of itself;   4. tRNA;   5. GCU and CGA;   6. RNA has U instead of T and it is single, not double stranded;   7. Store information/ instructions and to make copies of itself;   8. Only the 'sense' strand carries the 'message'. The other strand contains the complementary bases and has a different sequence.

Human insulin gene can be put into bacteria using genetic engineering

- Human cells with genes for healthy insulin are selected.
- A chromosome is removed from the cell.
- The insulin gene is cut from the chromosome using an enzyme.
- The selected bacterial cell would contain DNA in circular plasmids.
- All the plasmids are removed from the bacterial cell.
- The plasmids are cut open with the same enzyme.
- Human insulin gene is inserted into the plasmids.
- The plasmids are returned to the bacterial cell.
- The bacterial cell is allowed to reproduce as all of them contain human the insulin gene.
- As the bacterial cell reproduces it produces insulin which can be used by a diabetic person.

1. When testing for a faulty gene, state why the patient's DNA must be separated into a single strand.

1. A single strand is required so that the complementary strand on the gene probe can match.

KEY POINT Genetic engineering involves taking DNA from one organism and inserting it into the chromosomes of another organism.

The new organism then carries out the instructions on the new DNA. It works because all living organisms use the same code of four bases A, T, C and G in their DNA.

In other words *they all talk the same language.*

This means that a gene for making vitamin A in a carrot, will still make vitamin A if transferred to rice.

Many people in Asia eat mainly rice. Rice does not normally contain vitamin A. Lack of vitamin A causes damage to their eyes. Scientists have used genetic engineering to make a variety of rice that now makes vitamin A. Summary of this process is given below.

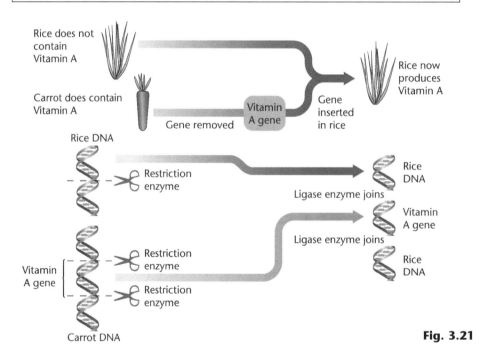

Fig. 3.21

The gene can be removed from the DNA by using **restriction enzymes** that cut the gene out of the DNA. The same enzymes can then be used to cut open the DNA of the new host organism. The new gene is inserted and another enzyme called a **ligase** is used to join the DNA back together.

KEY POINT Genetically modified foods or GM food has been genetically engineered by inserting a new gene from another organism. In other words, their DNA has been modified.

The rice that can produce vitamin A and save the sight of millions of people is an example of a genetically modified food.

Another example of GM food is 'GM soya bean'. The soyabean has been modified to be resistant to a special type of weed killer. This enables farmers to spray the soya bean with weed-killer to kill weeds without harming the soyabean. It also means that agro-chemical companies make large profits as the farmers not only buy the seed from them, but the weed-killer as well.

> This makes it easier for the farmer but may encourage a greater use of weed-killer.

The ethics of genetic engineering

> Some people are in favour of genetic engineering. They think the benefits will be enormous and worth the risks involved.
>
> Some people are against genetic engineering. They think the risks are too great and that we should not 'play around with nature'.

Benefits:

- cures for diseases, such as cystic fibrosis and cancer

- food which is healthier, stays fresh for longer periods and tastes better.

Risks:

- unknown effects of moving genes from one organism to the other

- new dangerous diseases being created

- against God and nature.

> This is part of the syllabus where you could be asked 'Ideas and Evidence' type questions, i.e. *What do you think and why?*

What do you think?

- Some people think that genetic engineering is against 'God and Nature' and is potentially dangerous.

- Some people think that genetic engineering will provide massive benefits to mankind, like better food and less disease.

PROGRESS CHECK

1. State one example of useful genetic engineering.
2. Name the enzymes that cut and join DNA together.
3. State one example of genetic engineering that might not be in the consumer's interest.
4. State which type of individuals will have the same genetic fingerprint.

1. Insertion of the vitamin A gene into rice to prevent eye diseases in people living in Asia; 2. Restriction enzymes cut and ligase enzymes join; 3. Making soyabeans resistant to weed-killer; 4. Identical twins.

Sample IGCSE questions

1.

(a) John could roll his tongue, but his sister, Jane could not. John's mother could roll her tongue but his father could not. Complete the following genetic diagram, to show the genotypes of John's family. **[4]**

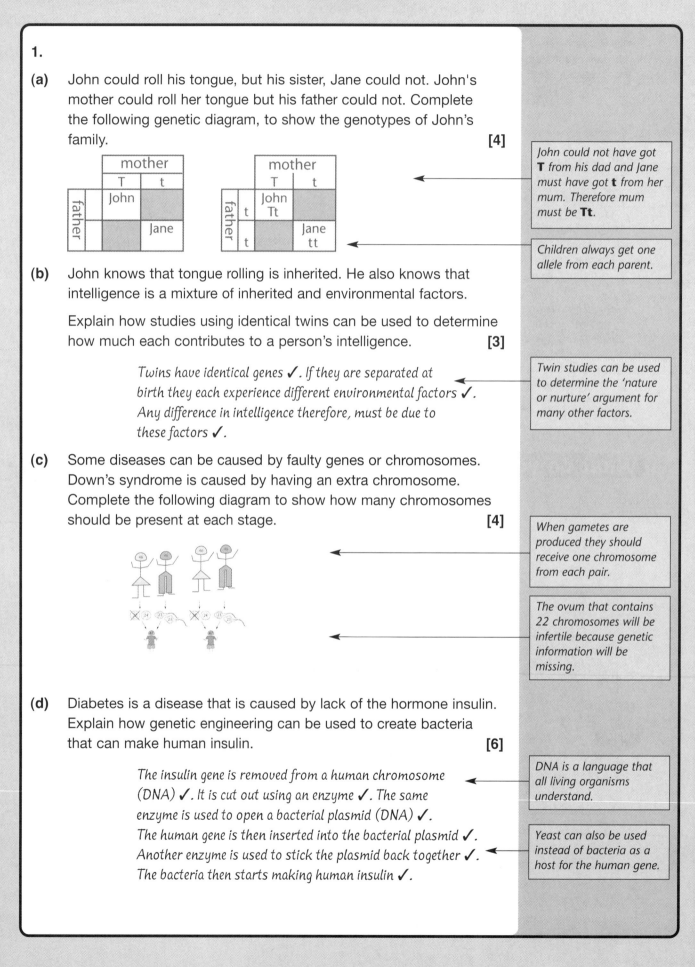

> *John could not have got **T** from his dad and Jane must have got **t** from her mum. Therefore mum must be **Tt**.*

> *Children always get one allele from each parent.*

(b) John knows that tongue rolling is inherited. He also knows that intelligence is a mixture of inherited and environmental factors.

Explain how studies using identical twins can be used to determine how much each contributes to a person's intelligence. **[3]**

Twins have identical genes ✓. If they are separated at birth they each experience different environmental factors ✓. Any difference in intelligence therefore, must be due to these factors ✓.

> *Twin studies can be used to determine the 'nature or nurture' argument for many other factors.*

(c) Some diseases can be caused by faulty genes or chromosomes. Down's syndrome is caused by having an extra chromosome. Complete the following diagram to show how many chromosomes should be present at each stage. **[4]**

> *When gametes are produced they should receive one chromosome from each pair.*

> *The ovum that contains 22 chromosomes will be infertile because genetic information will be missing.*

(d) Diabetes is a disease that is caused by lack of the hormone insulin. Explain how genetic engineering can be used to create bacteria that can make human insulin. **[6]**

The insulin gene is removed from a human chromosome (DNA) ✓. It is cut out using an enzyme ✓. The same enzyme is used to open a bacterial plasmid (DNA) ✓. The human gene is then inserted into the bacterial plasmid ✓. Another enzyme is used to stick the plasmid back together ✓. The bacteria then starts making human insulin ✓.

> *DNA is a language that all living organisms understand.*

> *Yeast can also be used instead of bacteria as a host for the human gene.*

Exam practice questions

1. Following figure shows changes in the population of yeast during the production of beer.

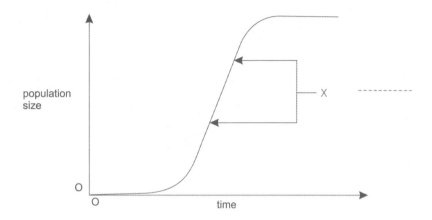

(a) **(i)** On the above figure name the phase labelled **X**. [2]

(ii) Suggest two reasons why the population stops growing.

1. ....

2. .... [2]

(b) Write an equation, in either words or chemical symbols, for anaerobic respiration by yeast

[2]

(c) Alcohol has long term effects that cause damage to some body organs.

Name two of these organs and state an effect that alcohol can have on each of these organs.

1 Organ...

Effect..

....

2 Organ...

Effect ....

.... [4]

Exam practice questions

2. The following figure shows the female reproductive system.

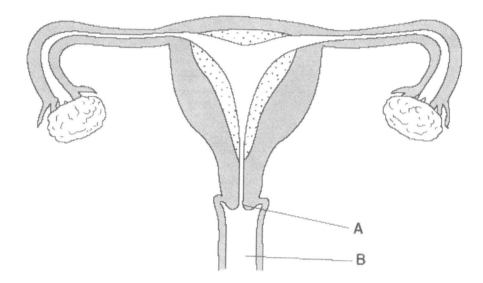

(a) Name the structures labelled A and B

A ....

B ....[2]

(b) Label, on Fig. 2.1, with the appropriate letter, where

    (i)   fertilisation   normally occurs – F   **[1]**

    (ii)   Gametes are produced   – G   **[1]**

    (iii)   oestrogen is produced   – O   **[1]**

(c) List three secondary sexual characteristics that are stimulated by oestrogen.

    1.   ....

    2.   ....

    3.   ....**[3]**

(d) Outline the changes occurring in the ovaries and uterus during the menstrual cycle.

....

....

....

....

Exam practice questions

....

....

....**[4]**

3. Plants need both magnesium ions and nitrate ions for healthy development.

    (i) State why each of these is important for healthy development.

    Magnesium ions ....

    ....

    Nitrate ions ....

    ....**[2]**

    (ii) Nitrate ions are often provided in fertilizers. Excess fertilizer may be washed into streams and ponds polluting the water. Suggest what is likely to happen in the stream or pond.

    ....

    ....

    ....

    ....

    ....

    ....**[4]**

    (iii) Use only words or letters from the list below to complete the sentence in the following paragraph.

Diploid,	Forty-four,	forty-six,	gamete,
haploid,	twenty-two,	twenty-three,	X, Y, zygote

    The nuclei of human body cells contain .... pairs of chromosomes, that is ....chromosomes and two sex chromosomes.

    Sperm cells have a .... nucleus with a single sex chromosome.

    The ....formed from the fusion of an ovum with a sperm cell, containing a...................sex chromosome, will develop into a male.   **[Total: 5]**

Chapter 4

Relationships of organisms with one another and with their environment

The following topics are covered in this section:

- **Energy flow**
- **Food chains and food webs**
- **Nutrient cycles**
- **Population size**
- **Human influences on the ecosystem**

4.1 Energy flow

LEARNING SUMMARY

After studying this section you should be able to:

- *state the role of the Sun in the biological system*
- *describe the non-cyclic nature of energy flow*
- *define the terms food chain, food web, producer, consumer, herbivore, carnivore, decomposer, ecosystem and trophic level*
- *describe energy losses between trophic levels*
- *describe and interpret pyramids of number, biomass and energy*
- *explain how energy is passed along food chains and is stored all along the chain*
- *realise that bacteria and fungi carry out an important job in decaying dead material*
- *understand how this decay allows minerals to be recycled in nature.*

Definitions

Food chain	–	passage of food (and therefore energy) from one organism to another
Food web	–	interlinking of food chains
Producer	–	organism which makes its own food using organic substance (photosynthesis)
Consumer	–	organism that obtains its food by feeding on other organisms
Herbivore	–	animals who eat only plants
Carnivore	–	animals who eat other animals
Decomposer	–	organism that obtains its food by breaking down dead organic matter
Ecosystem	–	a biotic community together with the physical (abiotic) environment
Trophic level	–	organism position in a food chain, food web or food pyramid

KEY POINT   **Sun provides us with heat and light.**

- Photosynthetic plants and some bacteria trap light energy and convert it into chemical energy.
- Heterotrophic organisms get energy from the photosynthetic plants or animals who have eaten plants.

KEY POINT   **All organisms get their energy from the Sun.**

- Energy is passed from one organism to another in a food chain.
- Unlike elements like C, N, O energy does not return in a cycle.

 KEY POINT   **Once energy lost is lost forever.**

Energy transfer

Food chain

A series of organisms arranged linearly such that each organism feeds on the one below the series, assuming that each organism feeds on only other type of organism.

Large carnivore 4th trophic level
▽
Carnivores 3rd trophic level
▽
Herbivores 2nd trophic level
▽
Producers 1st trophic level

Fig. 4.1

One-way grassland food chain

Flow of energy

Sun is the principal source of energy in biological systems.

Green plants absorb only a very small fraction (about 10%) of the solar energy incident on the Earth.

Solar energy converts into potential chemical energy (by plants).

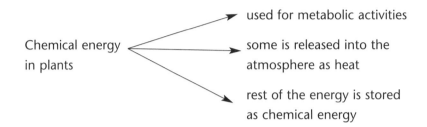

Chemical energy in plants
- used for metabolic activities
- some is released into the atmosphere as heat
- rest of the energy is stored as chemical energy

Ten percent law

Only 10% of the total energy entering a particular trophic level is available for transfer to the next higher trophic level, e.g.

Grass ⟶ Goat ⟶ Tiger
200 Kg   10%   20 Kg   10%   2 Kg

> **Energy flow is noncyclical**

So the increase in dry mass of tiger which will result from 200 Kg of grass will be 2 Kg.

- Short food chains provide more energy to the higher trophic level.
- In a five level food chain the last trophic level may not get any energy left for it.

> **KEY POINT** Vegetarians who eat plants get more energy than people eating pork or meat.

A food chain shows how food passes through a community of organisms. Food energy enters the food chain as sunlight is trapped by the producers. They use photosynthesis to trap the energy in the form of chemicals, such as sugars. The energy then passes from organism to organism as they eat each other.

> All the organisms in a food chain therefore rely on producers to trap the energy from the Sun.

Pyramid of Biomass

Biomass is the total dry mass of all organisms in a unit area.
Total biomass = Biomass of producers + Biomass of consumers + Biomass of decomposers.

The mass of all the organisms at each step of the food chain can be measured. On the basis of the measurement of dry mass at each trophic level, a diagram can be drawn, known as Pyramid of biomass.

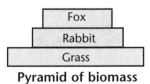

Pyramid of biomass

Fig. 4.2

Pyramid of numbers

This is drawn according to the number of organisms at each trophic level of the food chain.

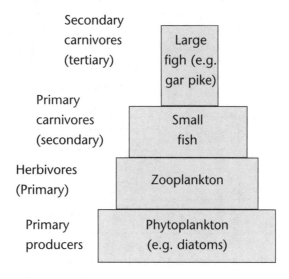

Secondary carnivores (tertiary) — Large figh (e.g. gar pike)

Primary carnivores (secondary) — Small fish

Herbivores (Primary) — Zooplankton

Primary producers — Phytoplankton (e.g. diatoms)

Fig. 4.3

Pyramid of numbers

The pyramid of biomass has some advantages and disadvantages over the pyramid of numbers:

Advantages:
● it takes into account the size of each organism, so it is a pyramid.

Disadvantages:
● it is harder to measure the mass of organisms than to count them
● to measure biomass the organism has to be killed and dried out.

Pyramid of energy

● Energy pyramids are formed by measuring the amount of energy available at each trophic level in the food chain.
● The energy is measured over a fixed period of time.
● A normal shaped pyramid is formed, known as Pyramid of energy.

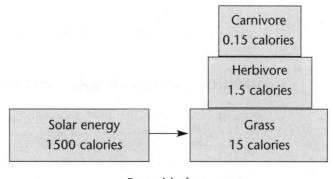

Carnivore 0.15 calories

Herbivore 1.5 calories

Solar energy 1500 calories → Grass 15 calories

Pyramid of energy

Fig. 4.4

Ecosystem

An **ecosystem** is an environment plus the living organisms within that environment.

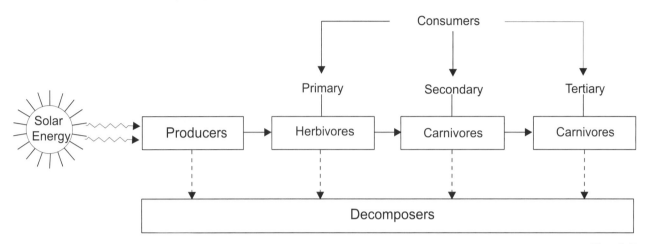

Schematic representation showing various structrural components of ecosystem.

Fig. 4.5

 KEY POINT Some ecosystems are natural, e.g. deserts, polar regions, oceans, tropical rain forests. Other ecosystems are man-made or artificial, e.g. fields, parks, built up areas.

Some ecosystems that we might think are natural, such as moorland and pine forests, are in fact artificial ecosystems. Pine forests are planted and grown for their wood and moorland is maintained for grouse shooting. A few hundred years ago, over 50% of England was covered by broad-leaf woodland. This figure is now less than 4%. Open hillsides are kept free of trees, by farmers grazing their sheep. If the environment was left alone, after a few years, it would revert back to broad-leaf woodland.

Species diversity index

 KEY POINT The variety of different species within an ecosystem is called diversity. The greater the number of species, the greater the diversity.

In other words, if one food source disappears, there will be plenty of other food available.

The greater the diversity within an ecosystem, the more stable and secure that ecosystem is.

The food web will be very large, so any change to one part of the web will make only a very small change to the whole ecosystem.

Species conservation – extinction is forever

Some species, such as the giant panda and the Indian tiger, are close to extinction.

Many zoos around the world have started breeding programmes to try to protect endangered species. However, it is only by protecting their natural environment that we can ensure their long-term survival. In Great Britain special environments can be protected by declaring them as SSSI or **Sites of Special Scientific Interest**. This protects the sites from further development. On a small scale, conservation can be carried out by:

● planting trees

● making new ponds and lakes

● putting up bird and bat boxes.

Aesthetic and cultural reasons

People enjoy visiting 'wild places' and seeing the variety of living things.

Conservation makes sense

Economic reasons

The genes of extinct organisms are fast.

When ecosystems collapse they can no longer be harvested.

Fig. 4.6

PROGRESS CHECK

1. Differentiate between producer and a consumer.
2. Name two things provided by the Sun.
3. What happens to the energy trapped by the plants from the Sun?
4. How much of solar energy is absorbed by the green plants?
5. Give the technical term for the total dry mass of all organisms in a unit area.
6. What do you understand by ten percent law?
7. Why is vegetarianism scientifically supported?

1. Organism which makes food with the help of inorganic materials and the organism which consumes or eats the food made by the producers; 2. Heat and light; 3. Converted into chemical energy. 4. Only 1% of the energy provided by the Sun is absorbed by the green plants for photosynthesis; 5. Biomass; 6. Only 10% of the total energy is available for transfer to the next trophic level; 7. According to the ten percent law, vegetarians get more energy compared to non-vegetarians, because they receive more energy from plants since they are the producers and belong to the first trophic level, whereas non-vegetarians consume the second level, thus receiving lesser amounts of energy.

4.2 Nutrient cycles

After studying this section you should be able to:

● describe carbon, nitrogen and water cycles
● explain the effects of burning and increase of CO_2 levels in the atmosphere
● discuss the balance between CO_2 and O_2 in the atmosphere.

Carbon cycle

It is possible to follow the way by which each mineral element passes through living organisms and becomes available again for use. Scientists use nutrient cycles to show how these minerals are recycled in nature.

 Carbon sources are not normally available to living organisms; they represent the main carbon reservoirs.

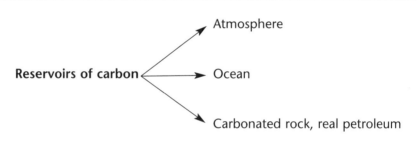

We may be risking major environmental change by adding carbon dioxide to the atmosphere at the present rates. Efforts are being made by governments to reduce the rate of use of fossil fuels by finding alternative sources of energy, such as solar or wind power.

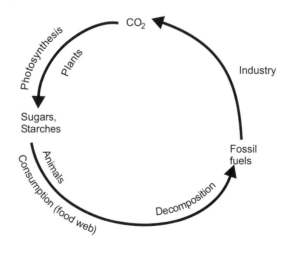

Carbon cycle

Fig. 4.7

Steps of the carbon cycle

- Most of the carbon dioxide enters the living world through the process of photosynthesis.

- Plants convert carbon dioxide into organic material (carbohydrates, fats and proteins).

- Herbivores get their CO_2 from plants.

- Both animals and plants release CO_2 through respiration.

- Plants and animals are broken down by decomposers when they die.

- Combustion of fossil fuels releases CO_2.

- So the carbon cycle operates in the biosphere ensuring the amount of carbon dioxide in the atmosphere remains almost the same.

> Records show that human activity has led to a marked build up of carbon dioxide in the atmosphere since the industrial revolution.

Nitrogen cycle

The nitrogen cycle is complicated because it involves three other types of bacteria as well as the decomposers :

- **nitrifying bacteria** – these bacteria live in the soil and convert ammonium compounds to nitrates. They need oxygen to do this

- **denitrifying bacteria** – these bacteria in the soil are the enemy of farmers. They turn nitrates into nitrogen gas. They do not need oxygen

- **nitrogen fixing bacteria** – they live in the soil or in nodules on the roots of plants from the pea and bean family. They take nitrogen gas and convert it back to useful nitrogen compounds.

> **KEY POINT** Nitrogen comprises of 78–79% of the earth's atmosphere.

> Nitrogen in the atmosphere cannot be absorbed by plants and animals directly.

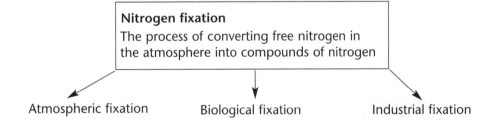

Nitrogen fixation
The process of converting free nitrogen in the atmosphere into compounds of nitrogen

Atmospheric fixation   Biological fixation   Industrial fixation

> **KEY POINT** All nitrogen-fixers incorporate nitrogen into ammonia, but this is immediately used to make organic compounds, mainly proteins.

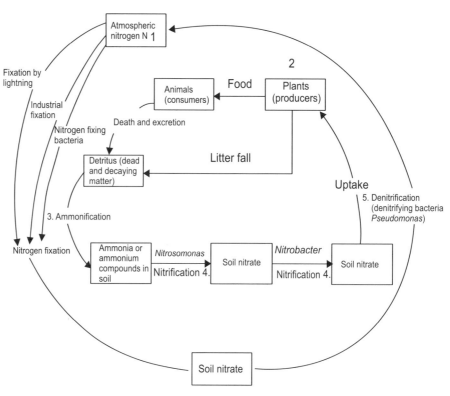

Nitrogen cycle.   **Fig. 4.8**

Atmosphere fixation

High temperature produced during lightning allows nitrogen to combine with
oxygen in the atmosphere to form oxides of nitrogen. This dissolves in rain and
falls on the Earth. This gets stored in the soil.

Water cycle

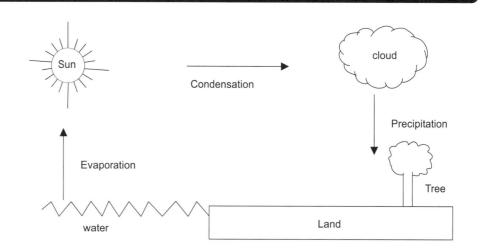

Water vapour in
the atmosphere is
an important green
house gas, like
carbon dioxide.

Steps of water cycle   **Fig. 4.9**

● Water evaporates due to the heat of the Sun from all the water bodies like
lakes, river, seas, ocean, etc.

● This vapour condenses in the form of precipitation (rain).

- The rain water fills up the streams, rivers, lakes, seas, etc.
- Plant roots take up water by osmosis, some of it is lost from leaves through transpiration.
- Animals also leave water into the environment through excretion, sweating and faeces.
- Drying of any organic matter gives off water vapour into the environment.

Balance between O_2 – CO_2 and the water cycle

Photosynthesis ⟶ takes in CO_2 and gives out O_2
Respiration ⟶ takes in O_2 and gives out CO_2
So these two processes have to be balanced for the balancing of oxygen and CO_2 in the environment.

The processes that change the equilibrium are:

(a) **deforestation**
(b) **combustion of fossil fuels.**

This means:

- more CO_2 in the atmosphere
- more deforestation
- more mining leading to habitat destruction
- increased number of animals
- more the population of men / animals
- more respiration so more CO_2
- more O_2 is utilised.

> **Human activity generally speeds up movement of material through the cycles and may fundamentally upset the balance of cycles**

Effects of increase in CO_2 levels

reduces rainfall, leads to desert formation

melts polar ice caps, can flood low lying areas or coastal areas

Increase in CO_2 levels

can lead to mass-extinction due to climatic changes

> **Carbon dioxide concentration in the atmosphere varies between 0.03% and 0.04%, but increases in photosynthetic rate can be achieved by increasing this percentage.**

Relationships of organisms with one another and with their environment

PROGRESS
CHECK

1. What are the reservoirs of carbon?
2. Match the following

    (a) oxygen   rhizobium

    (b) leguminous plants   evaporation

    (c) carbon dioxide   by product of photosynthesis

    (d) sunlight   green house effect

3. What is conversion of ammonia into nitrates called?
4. What do you understand by biogeochemical cycle?
5. What is biological fixation of nitrogen?
6. How is the balance between carbon dioxide and oxygen maintained in the atmosphere?
7. What are the effects of increase in the levels of carbon dioxide?

1. Rocks, oceans, atmosphere; 2. (a) oxygen — by-product of photosynthesis; (b) leguminous plants — rhizobium; (c) carbon dioxide — green house effect; (d) sunlight — evaporation; 3. Nitrification; 4. The cyclic pathway of mineral nutrients from abiotic to the biotic world; 5. The fixation of nitrogen by bacteria and blue green algae is called biological fixation; 6. Carbon dioxide is given out as respiration by every living organism, which is used up by the plants for the process of photosynthesis; 7. Global warming leading to desertification, melting of ice caps, floods.

4.3 Population Size

LEARNING SUMMARY

After studying this section you should be able to:

● *state the factors affecting the rate of population growth and describe its importance*
● *identify sigmoid curve*
● *describe the social implication of current human survival rate.*

Population

Population is a group of one species of organisms living in the same place.

The number of humans living on Earth has been increasing for a long time but it is going up more rapidly than ever before.

KEY POINT — **This increase is called a population explosion.**

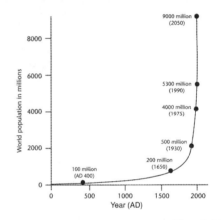

Fig. 4.10

Rate of the population growth

Food supply: More food allows animals to breed. Shortage of food may lead to migration or death due to starvation.

These factors can check the rate of population growth

Predation: Increase in predation ⟶ population will reduce
If predation decreases ⟶ population will increase

Disease: Diseases spread easily in populated areas. Epidemics can reduce population size very rapidly.

Contraceptives: Used by humans to reduce the population.

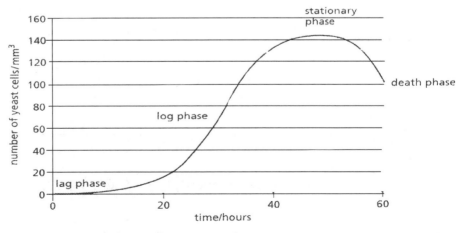

Different phases of population growth – sigmoid curve

Fig. 4.11

173

This is an **S-shaped** or **logistic growth curve**. It was described by **Verhulst**.

Lag phase – large increase in the population

Log phase – organisms continue to grow but at a steady rate

Stationary phase – population looses to grow
                                    reproduction rate = mortality rate

Death phase – population starts to decline

Human Population growth

Human population has been growing tremendously and traditionally it is accepted that disease, famine or war are factors causing it to decline. The current growth of population is driven by fertility. More developed countries have lower fertility rates than less developed countries.

 KEY POINT For population growth birth rate must be higher than death rate.

Population growth involves:

- less infant mortality
- increase in life expectancy
- increased survival rate
- availability of medical facilities.

Population pressure

More people – more agriculture
             – more industrialisation   lead to increase in pollution
             – more urbanisation   of air, land, water

Populations grow and decline in characteristic ways. The size of population is determined by the reproductive potential of the organisms and environmental resistance. The maximum reproductive potential is the rate of reproduction shown in unlimited environmental resources. Following shows the different patterns of human population growth in different countries.

Post-reproductive

Reproductive

Pre-reproductive

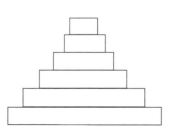
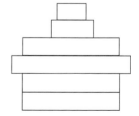

Expanding population   **Stable population**   **Declining population**

Fig. 4.12

Diagrams of human population growth

In many countries, doctors are trying to reduce the population explosion by educating people about contraception.

The increasing size of the human population means that there is a greater demand for land.

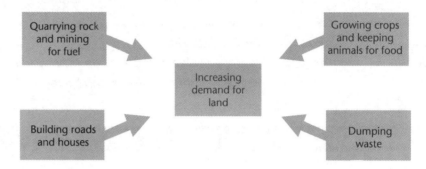

Quarrying rock and mining for fuel

Growing crops and keeping animals for food

Increasing demand for land

Building roads and houses

Dumping waste

Fig. 4.13

This increased demand for land and resources means that many organisms are decreasing in number. This is because:

Animals have been over-hunted for food

The habitats of many organisms have been disappeared

Harmful chemicals have killed organisms

Fig. 4.14

PROGRESS CHECK

1. State the factors on which population growth depends on.
2. Why has the death rate decreased in developing countries?
3. What is meant by population pressure?
4. What would be the effect of overpopulation?

1. Diseases, predation, food supply; 2. Due to better facilities of health, nutrition, housing facilities and education; 3. Population pressure indicates the effect of high numbers of people on the environment, greater food production, better housing and industries; 4. Increased pollution of land, water, and air, more food production leading to greater use of fertilisers. Greater urbanisation, road and house building.

4.4 Agriculture

After studying this section you should be able to:
- discuss the ways in which the use of modern technology has resulted in increased food production
- describe the undesirable effects of deforestation
- describe the overuse of fertilisers on the land.

Increased food production

Food production has increased tremendously because of the following reasons:

- use of chemical fertilisers increases the levels of nutrients in soil and crop yields
- pesticides and insecticides are used to kill pests that feed on crops and damage increased yields
- herbicides kill weeds that compete with crops
- modern machinery enables to manage crops more efficiently
- artificial selection to produce desired variety has increased the crop produce quality and quantity
- use of yeast, bacteria in food industry
- use of medicines, vaccinations
- artificial insemination to increase animal production
- application of genetic engineering
- application of hydroponics
- use of satellites to monitor crops.

Deforestation

Removal of large areas of forest for various reasons like:

It has been estimated that twelve million hectares of forest, an area of the size of England, are disappearing annually.

- farming
- industrialisation
- urbanisation
- timber collection.

Overuse of fertilisers

Modern intensive farming methods only work because of the use of fertilisers.

Growing crops in the same field for year after year will inevitably remove nutrients from the soil. These have to be replaced by using fertilisers. The use of fertilisers, particularly nitrates, leads to much greater crop production.

> **KEY POINT** Most fertilisers contain nitrates, phosphates and potassium. They are known as NPK fertilisers.

However their use have these following disadvantages:

- **soil structure** – organic fertilisers, such as manure, add humus to the soil. This gives the soil a good crumb structure. Inorganic fertilisers do not add humus and crumb structure deteriorates.
- **pollution of rivers** – the mineral salts are often washed out of the soil and into rivers. This can lead to **eutrophication**.

Eutrophication causes the death of fish due to oxygen shortage. This is how it works:

1. fertilisers get leached or washed into rivers
2. fertilisers cause a rapid growth of algae in rivers
3. only those algae near the surface get light and survive; the rest of the algae are starved of light and die
4. bacteria grow on the dead algae and cause them to rot
5. this leads to a rapid growth in the number of bacteria
6. bacteria need oxygen to grow and use it all up
7. thus fish do not get enough oxygen and die.

> Candidates usually do not do well on questions about eutrophication. You should learn these seven key points.

PROGRESS CHECK

1. State two advantages of using fertilisers.
2. State two disadvantages of using fertilisers.
3. Explain how using fertilisers can lead to eutrophication.
4. What new methods are used to improve crop production?
5. List any four effects of deforestation.
6. What happens to soil if we use sodium nitrate fertiliser regularly?

1. Increased crop production and using the same land over and over again; 2. Poor crumb structure and eutrophication; 3. Fertilisers leach or get washed into rivers. Fertilisers cause a rapid growth of algae in rivers. Only algae near the surface get light and survive. The rest of the algae are starved of light and die. Bacteria grow on the dead algae and cause them to rot. This leads to a rapid growth in the number of bacteria. The bacteria need oxygen to grow and use it all up. Fish do not have enough oxygen and die. 4. Chemical fertilisers, herbicides, pesticides, latest equipment, and new technologies. 5. Less rain, increase in soil erosion, oxygen depletion, increase in carbon dioxide levels. 6. The alkalinity of the soil increases.

4.5 Pollution

LEARNING SUMMARY

After studying this section you should be able to:

● describe the undesirable effects of water pollution
● describe the effects of air pollution
● explain the effects of pollution due to pesticides and herbicides
● assess the significance of non-biodegradable plastic
● discuss the effects of acid rain and ways to prevent/control it.

Modern methods of food production and the increasing demand for energy have caused many different types of **pollution**.

> **KEY POINT**
> Pollution is the release of substances that harm organisms into the environment.

The following table shows some of the main polluting substances that are being released into the environment.

Polluting substance	Main source	Effects on the environment
carbon dioxide	burning fossil fuels	greenhouse effect
carbon monoxide	car fumes	reduces oxygen carriage in the blood
fertilisers	intensive farming	*eutrophication*
heavy metals	factory waste	brain damage and death
herbicides	intensive farming	some cause mutations
methane	cattle and rice fields	greenhouse effect
sewage	human and farm waste	*eutrophication*
smoke	burning waste and fuel	smog and lung problems
sulphur dioxide	burning fossil fuels	*acid rain*

The **greenhouse effect** is caused by a build-up of certain gases, such as carbon dioxide and methane, in the atmosphere. These gases trap the heat rays as they are radiated from the Earth. This causes the Earth to warm up. This is similar to what happens in a greenhouse.

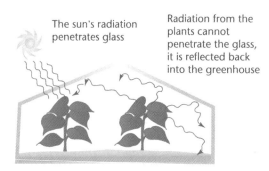

The sun's radiation penetrates glass

Radiation from the plants cannot penetrate the glass, it is reflected back into the greenhouse

Fig. 4.15   Green house

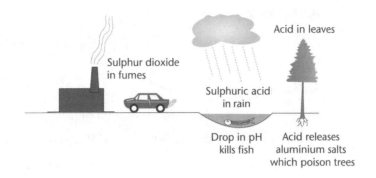

Fig. 4.16

Some organisms need lower amounts of oxygen to survive than others. The variety of organisms that is found in a river can be used to assess how polluted the river is.

Water pollution

1. can lead to diseases such as typhoid, cholera

2. can cause eutrophication

3. poisonous chemicals added to water can cause many diseases.

Air Pollution

can be caused due to:

1. smoke

2. particulates

3. sulphur dioxide

4. oxides of nitrogen

5. smog

6. carbon monoxide

7. chlorofluro carbons.

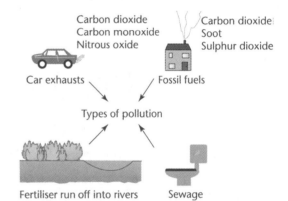

Fig. 4.17

Radioactivity and electromagnetic pulses may also pollute the atmosphere.

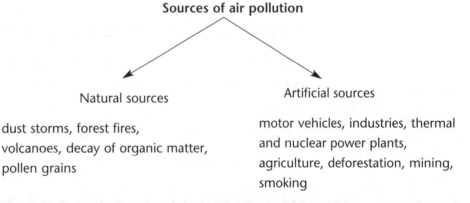

Sources of air pollution

Natural sources

dust storms, forest fires, volcanoes, decay of organic matter, pollen grains

Artificial sources

motor vehicles, industries, thermal and nuclear power plants, agriculture, deforestation, mining, smoking

Air pollution by sulphur dioxide

- Sulphur is found as impurity in coal and oil. So when these are burned sulphur dioxide is release into the air.

- Sulphur dioxide combines with water vapour in the cloud to form sulphuric acid.

- When these clouds fall as rain it becomes acidic in nature.

Acid rain

Acid rain is caused when the impurity sulphur, which is found in fossil fuels, is burned.

Steps

- Coal and oil contain sulphur as impurity.
- When these are burned sulphur is released as its oxide into air.
- The sulphur dioxide and water together form sulphuric acid.

> Acid rainfall (pH less than 5) often causes major changes in ecosystems and damage to buildings.

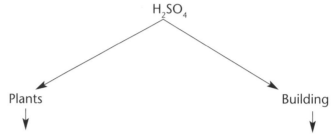

H_2SO_4

Plants → reduces the growth and damages leaves

Building → slowly dissolves limestone and mortar

> **KEY POINT**
>
> **Sulphur burns with oxygen to form sulphur dioxide.**
> $$S + O_2 \rightarrow SO_2$$

- The sulphur dioxide dissolves in rain to form acid rain.
- Nitrous oxide from car exhausts can also form acid rain.
- Acid rain reacts with buildings made from limestone.
- It kills trees and turns lakes acidic, thus killing fish.

Measures to reduce the effect of acid rain

More efficient use of fossil fuels means less acid rain. Efficiency can reduce the emissions that cause acid rain. We can all contribute with:

> Acid rainfall in central Sweden and southern Norway has affected salmon and trout fisheries.

- car pools
- improvement and increased use of mass transport
- proper maintenance of vehicles and pollution control devices.

Nuclear fallout can happen due to leakage from a nuclear power plant or nuclear explosion

- Radioactive particles are carried by wind/water to different places.
- These are absorbed by living organisms causing bioaccumulation.
- Accumulated radioactive substances are not excreted easily.
- This can cause cancer.

Pollution due to pesticides and herbicides

Some pesticides are non-biodegradable and stay in the environment.

- They travel up the food chain.
- They get accumulated in the top carnivores.

Herbicides are used to kill weeds.

- These are used to reduce competition among the different plants in a field and to increase crop yield.
- These may also kill rare plant species near the field.

Harmful effects of non-biodegradable plastics

- Plastics mostly are non-biodegradable.
- They remain in the environment as they cannot be decomposed by decomposers.
- They cause visual pollution.
- When used as land fills they can stop the growth of roots.
- Gradually they become a breeding ground for insects and spread diseases.

1. What are the two types of pollutants?
2. Name any two harmful effects of air pollution.
3. What is acid rain?
4. How are pesticides harmful?

PROGRESS CHECK

1. Biodegradable, non-biodegradable.
2. Breathing difficulties, carbon monoxide suffocation, acid rain, depletion of ozone layer, green house effect.
3. The rain which contains dissolved acids of sulphur and nitrogen.
4. Most of the pesticides are non-biodegradable and so they travel up the food chains and cause harm to organisms.

4.6 Conservation

LEARNING SUMMARY

After studying this section you should be able to:

● *know that many species of animals and plants are in danger of extinction*
● *know that species may play an important role in a food chain, its loss could endanger other species.*

Need for conservation

Many people believe that it is wrong for humans to damage natural habitats and cause the death of animals and plants. There are many reasons given, such as:

● extinct organisms may have unexpected effects on the environment, such as the erosion caused by deforestation

● people enjoy seeing different animals and plants

● some organisms may prove to be useful in the future, for breeding, producing important drugs or for their genes

● humans do not have a right to wipe out other species.

> **KEY POINT**
> • Using laws to protect habitats
> • Using wardens to protect habitats
> • Controlling public access to habitats

> **KEY POINT**
> Many people are trying to preserve habitats and keep all species of organisms alive. This is called conservation.

Conservation can be helped by adopting the 'three R's': Reduce, Re-use and Recycle.

Fig. 4.18

To be able to save habitats and organisms, people must find methods of meeting the ever increasing demand for food and energy, without causing pollution or over-exploitation.

> **KEY POINT**
> This environmentally friendly growth is called sustainable development.

In 1992, over 150 nations attended a meeting in Brazil called the **Earth Summit**. They agreed on ways in which countries could work together to achieve sustainable development.

local agenda 21

Fig. 4.19

They agreed to:

● reduce pollution from chemicals such as carbon dioxide. This can be done by cutting down on the waste of energy or by using sources of energy that do not produce carbon dioxide.

● reduce hunting of certain animals, such as whales.

The document that they signed was called **Agenda 21** and local governments are being encouraged to set up local schemes to help in conservation.

Sewage treatment

Sewage is made up of a number of different components but includes toilet flushings, kitchen waste and water from washing. This is mixed with some industrial waste, which by law has to receive some treatment before it is allowed to enter the sewers.

> **KEY POINT** Sewage is treated to make it safe by using microbes to break down the organic substances.

Proper sewage treatment is important for two main reasons:
- it removes pathogens and so stops them infecting other people
- it allows the water to be released into rivers without the dangers of eutrophication.

There are two main types of sewage treatment:
- **biological filter** (trickling filter): this involves trickling the sewage through a bed of stones that are coated with a community of microbes. The microbes breakdown and feed on the organic matter
- **activated sludge**: this can deal with larger amounts of sewage and involves adding microbes to the sewage. It is then held in large tanks whilst air is bubbled through.

Both processes rely on the sewage being allowed to settle first so that the larger particles are removed as sludge.

Notice that this process makes some fertiliser and the fuel methane as well as clean water.

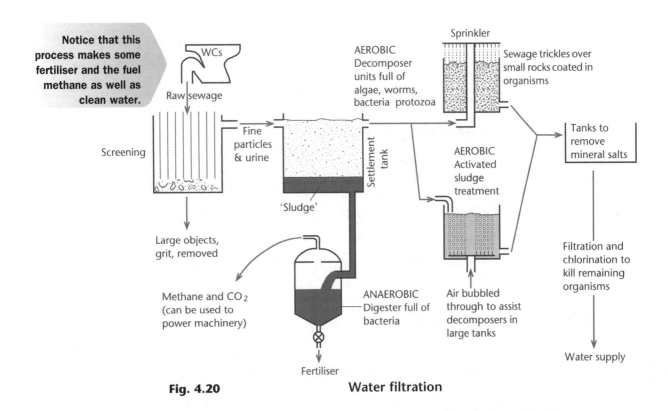

Fig. 4.20 **Water filtration**

Water filtration

> In places where there is shortage of water sewage water is treated to provide water which is clean enough to drink.

Process

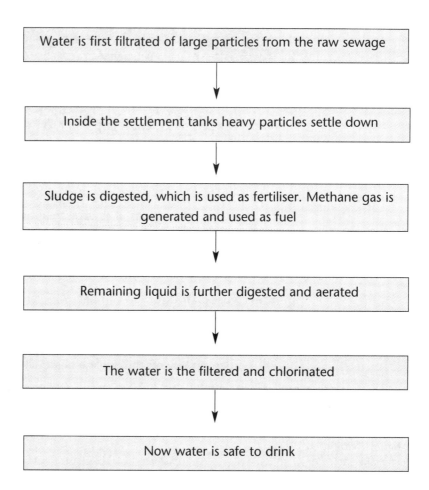

Water is first filtrated of large particles from the raw sewage

↓

Inside the settlement tanks heavy particles settle down

↓

Sludge is digested, which is used as fertiliser. Methane gas is generated and used as fuel

↓

Remaining liquid is further digested and aerated

↓

The water is the filtered and chlorinated

↓

Now water is safe to drink

Recycling of paper

- Paper is made from wood.
- After use of paper it can be made into pulp.
- Any ink or dyes are removed then.
- The pulp can then be rolled into sheets and dried.
- These sheets can be used as newspaper, toilet paper, hard towel, etc.

1. What is a rapid increase in the size of a population called?
2. Write down three things that an increasing population needs.
3. Write down the name of each of these polluting substances:
    (a) a chemical added to crops to supply minerals
    (b) a chemical that causes acid rain
    (c) a gas given off by burning fuels that may cause the greenhouse effect.
4. When a pond suffers from eutrophication, why do most of the organisms die?
5. Name an animal that man has hunted to extinction.
6. Write down two reasons why rainforests are being cut down and two effects that might have on the environment.
7. How does recycling glass bottles help to save energy?
8. Differentiate between producer and consumer.
9. Name two things provided by the Sun.
10. What happens to the energy trapped by the plants from the Sun?
11. How much of solar energy is absorbed by the green plants?
12. Give the technical term for the total dry mass of all organisms in a unit area.
13. What do you understand by 10% law?
14. Why is vegetarianism scientifically supported?
15. Name two things which can be recycled?
16. Why should we protect habitats?
17. What is the advantage of sewage treatment?
18. How is paper recycled?

1. A population explosion; 2. More food, shelter and clothes;
3. (a) Fertilisers (b) Sulphur dioxide; (c) Carbon dioxide; 4. They lack oxygen;
5. The Dodo or Great Auk ; 6. Room to farm, for timber, to build houses, roads; this may lead to soil erosion; 7. It reduces the amount of energy and raw materials used to make new glass.
8. Organism which makes food with the help of inorganic materials and the organism which consumes or eats the food made by the producers. 9. Heat and light. 10. Converted into chemical energy. 11. Only 1% of the energy provided by the Sun is absorbed by the green plants for photosynthesis. 12. Biomass. 13. Only 10% of the total energy is available for transfer to the next trophic level. 14. According to the 10 percent law, vegetarians would get more energy compared to non-vegetarians as they are getting more energy from plants since they are the producers and belong to the first trophic level whereas non-vegetarians are eating the second level, receiving lesser amounts of energy. 15. Paper, metal. 16. To protect all types of wildlife and their environment. 17. Sewage treatment prevents pollution, provides water for use. 18. Paper is made into pulp, colours are removed, rolled out into sheets and used.

Sample IGCSE questions

1. Bunti went on a Field Trip. He identified and counted the types of organisms in a fresh water stream. He completed the following table.

Animal name	Score	✓ if found
Shrimp	6	✓
Caddis	7	✓
Pond skater	5	
Water boatman	5	
Water beetle	5	✓
Midge larvae	2	✓
TOTAL		

This is calculating a simple biotic index.

(a) (i) Calculate the total score. [1]

30 ✓

(ii) State how many different species Bunti found. [1]

4 ✓

(iii) Bunti then calculated the Species Diversity Index.

Explain what this would tell Bunti about the stream. [3]

The greater number of species, ✓ the higher the diversity, ✓ the less polluted is the stream ✓.

It would be easy to answer this question by saying "the more species ✓, the less pollution ✓", but this would only get two marks. This is why it is important to look to see how many marks the question is worth.

(b) Bunti tested the acidity of the river and found it is acidic at pH6.

He thought it might be caused by acid rain.

(i) State the name of one chemical that causes acid rain. [1]

Sulphur dioxide ✓.

(ii) Explain where this chemical may have come from. [1]

Burning fossil fuels that contain sulphur ✓.

(c) The teacher told Bunti that plans existed to build a factory close to the river.

(i) State two groups that might be affected if the factory was built. [2]

Local residents ✓ and developers ✓.

(ii) An Environmental Impact Statement had been produced for the new factory. Explain the purpose of the statement. [3]

To inform ✓ people about the impact ✓ of the development so that a decision ✓ could be made.

Ideas and Evidence type of question. It also includes aspects of citizenship that you will consider in many other subject areas.

Exam practice questions

1. **The following shows a food web from farmland in Europe.**

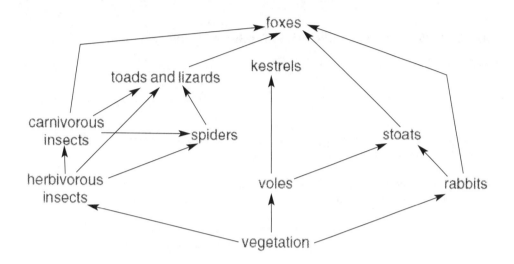

(a) (i) Name an organism from the fourth trophic level of this food web.

.... [1]

(ii) Using examples from this food web explain the difference between primary and secondary consumers.

....

....

....

.... [4]

(b) (i) State the source of energy for this food web.

.... [1]

(ii) In the food web the herbivorous insect population receives the same total amount of energy as the rabbit population. The rabbits pass a smaller percentage of this total energy to the next trophic level compared with the herbivorous insects. Explain the reason for this.

Exam practice answers

Chapter 1 Characteristics and classification of living organisms

1 (a) A = plant
   B = plant
   C = fungi
   D = plant
   E = protoctista [5]
   (b) Feeds on dead [1] organic material [1] releasing enzymes onto the food [1]
   (c) Animals [1] bacteria [1]

2 (a) Uses a single characteristic to classify organisms [1]
   (b) (i)   Gives organisms two Latin names [1], first is the genus, second is the species [1]
       (ii) before then organisms had common names [1], different organisms may have had the same name [1] or one organism may have had different names in different areas [1]
   (c) People travelled more widely during Ray and Linnaeus's time [1], improved communication systems [1] improved documentation [1]

Chapter 2 Organisation and maintenance of the organism

1 (a) 1250 [2]
       1 mark if working out shown but answer wrong
   (b) (i)   Same as body temperature [1]
       (ii) Protein [1]
       (iii) Molecules too large to pass through in the membrane [1]
   (c) Red blood cells carry oxygen from the lungs to the tissues[1] and white blood cells protect us from disease. [1]
   (d) (i)   Kidney machines do not operate for twenty four hours a day, blood has to be returned from the machine at body temperature, blood has to be prevented from clotting while in the machine, cross contamination has to be prevented. [3]
       (ii) Answers will vary but should show some understanding of the tissues involved. [3]

2 (a) (i)   Cytoplasm, chloroplast, vacuole and cell wall should be correctly labelled. [4]
       (ii) The leaf
       (iii) Any two from: chloroplast, cell wall, vacuole [2]
   (b) The possible answers are: mitochondria, ribosomes, endoplasmic reticulum [1]

3 (a) Minerals are taken up by active transport [1] this requires energy from respiration [1] respiration requires oxygen [1]
   (b) Increased oxygen in the soil [1] therefore more mineral uptake [1] so plants grow faster. [1]

Chapter 3 Development of the organism and the continuity of life

1 (a) (i)   labeled log/logarithmic/exponential phase:

(ii)   1. too little food materials/nutrients/sugar/glucose:

2. (build up) of waste/toxic products/alcohol/ethanol:

(b) $L_6H_{12}O_6 \xrightarrow[\text{fermentation}]{\text{alcoholic}} 2C_2H_5OH + 2CO_2 \uparrow$

(c) Organ: Liver;
   Effect: destroys/ damages cells/causes cirrhosis/impairs functions.
   Organ: Brain;
   Effect: destroys damages cells/impairs functions/named function/slows
        impulses/reactions;

2 (a) A – cervix;
   B – Vagina/birth canal; **[2]**

(b) (i)   F – label indicating cavity of oviduct;
   (ii)   G – label indicating ovary;
   (iii)   O – label indicating ovary

(c) widening of hips
   development of breasts/mammary glands;
   growth of public/auxillary hair; **[3]**

(d) shedding of uterine lining/menstruation/(menstrual) period;
   build up of new lining;
   maturing of ovum;
   ovulation;
   vascularisation/maintenance of lining;
   breakdown of lining if ovum not fertilized/no breakdown if ovum fertilized; **[4]**

3 (i)   magnesium needed to make chlorophyll;
   nitrates needed to make amino acids/protein/enzymes/DNA; **[2]**

(ii) increased growth of algae/aquatic plants;
   covers water surface/blocks entry of light;
   underwater plants etc. die;
   (decay) bacteria/decomposers increase;
   use up oxygen;
   water becomes anaerobic;
   aquatic animals die/migrate;
   eutrophication; **[4]**

(iii) twenty-three/23
   forty-four/44
   haploid;
   zygote;
   Y; **[5]**

Chapter 4 Relationships of organisms with one another and
with their environment

1 (a) (i)   Foxes   **[1]**
   (ii)   Primary consumers are herbivorous whereas secondary consumers are
        carnivorous.   **[4]**
(b) (i)   Source of energy: Sun   **[1]**
   (ii)   Rabbits are mammals and require more energy for respiration.   **[3]**

International General Certificate of Secondary Education

Model Test Paper I
BIOLOGY

M.M: 90   **Time: 1 hour 15 min**

SECTION-A

[Each question carries 1 mark]

1   Which activities are carried out by **all** living things?

   A   excreting, growing, reproducing, respiring

   B   excreting, moving, reproducing, sleeping

   C   growing, moving, respiring, thinking

   D   growing, respiring, swimming, thinking

2   An organism has a segmented body, pairs of jointed legs and a hard exoskeleton (outer covering).

   To which group does it belong?

   A   annelids

   B   arthropods

   C   molluscs

   D   nematodes

3   Use the key to identify this animal.

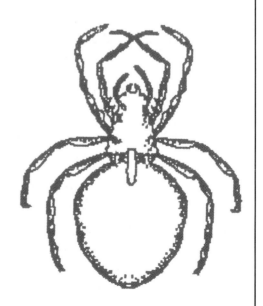

1 legs present .... go to 2

   legs absent... **A**

2 five pairs of legs .... **B**

   four pairs of legs .... go to 3

3 two body sections .... **C**

   three body sections .... **D**

4 Which parts are found both in plant and in animal cells?

   A cell membrane, chloroplast, vacuole

   B cell membrane, cytoplasm, nucleus

   C cell wall, chloroplast, cytoplasm

   D cell wall, nucleus, vacuole

5 The diagram shows some internal parts of the human body.

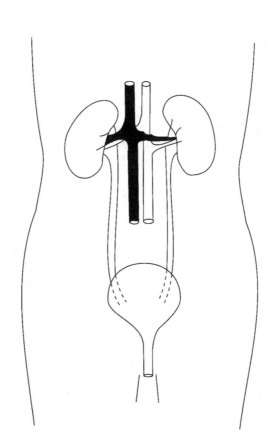

What do these parts form?

   A an organ

   B an organism

   C an organ system

   D a tissue

6   The diagram shows four different cells (not drawn to scale).

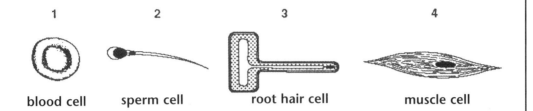

| 1 | 2 | 3 | 4 |
| blood cell | sperm cell | root hair cell | muscle cell |

Which cells provide a large surface area for absorption?

A   1 and 2   B   1 and 3   C   2 and 4   D   3 and 4

7   The following diagram shows a plant cell before and after being placed in a
sugar solution for ten minutes.

What describes the concentration of the sugar solution compared with that
of the cell sap and the type of molecules moving into the cell?

	concentration of sugar solution compared with cell sap	molecules moving into the cell
A	higher	sugar
B	higher	water
C	lower	sugar
D	lower	water

8   Why are all gaseous exchange surfaces moist?

   A   concentration gradients occur only in liquids

   B   gases dissolve before diffusing across the surfaces

   C   gases move across the surfaces by osmosis

   D   molecules cannot diffuse in air

9   The table shows two properties of four different chemicals.

Which chemical is an enzyme?

chemical	molecular structure includes nitrogen	destroyed by temperatures above 65 °C
A	✓	✓
B	✓	✗
C	✗	✓
D	✗	✗

key

✓ = true

✗ = false

10   The apparatus shown in the diagram was used for an experiment on starch digestion.

Which tube would contain most maltose after 20 minutes?

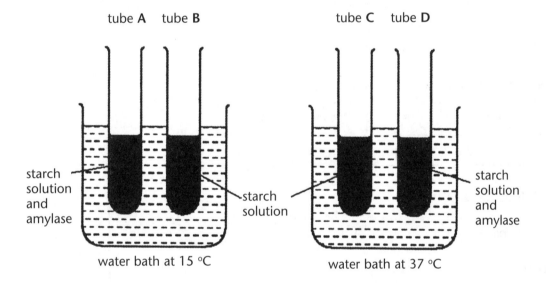

11   The equation represents a process that occurs in plants.

carbon dioxide + water ⟶ glucose + oxygen

What is the name of this process?

A   evaporation

B   photosynthesis

C   respiration

D   transpiration

12 What is carried by the phloem?

A chlorophyll

B mineral salts

C starch

D sugar

13 How is the rate of transpiration affected by increasing humidity and by increasing light intensity?

	increasing humidity	increasing light intensity
A	decreases	decreases
B	decreases	increases
C	increases	decreases
D	increases	increases

14 The table shows the results of food tests carried out on a fruit.

test	Benedict's	biuret	ethanol	iodine
result	positive	positive	negative	negative

What did the fruit contain?

A fat and reducing sugar

B fat and starch

C protein and reducing sugar

D protein and starch

15 Why is iron needed by the body?

A to form strong bones

B to make haemoglobin

C to provide energy

D to repair cells

16 Four foods were analysed to discover their chemical structure.

Which food is an oil?

	food			
	A	**B**	**C**	**D**
contains the elements carbon, hydrogen and oxygen	✓	✓	✓	✗
contains the elements carbon, hydrogen, oxygen and nitrogen	✗	✗	✗	✓
made up of amino acids	✗	✗	✗	✓
made up of fatty acids and glycerol	✓	✗	✗	✗
storage compound in plants	✓	✓	✗	✗
storage compound in animals	✓	✗	✓	✗

key

✓ = true

✗ = false

17 What is the most likely cause of a heart attack?

A blocked coronary arteries

B diet lacking in vitamins C and D

C infection by microorganisms

D regular exercise

18 The graph shows a person's heart rate before, during and after a period of exercise.

At which point did the period of exercise stop?

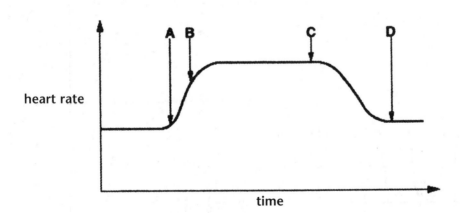

19 Why is yeast used in breadmaking?

A to produce alcohol

B to produce carbon dioxide

C to use up oxygen

D to use up sugar

20 The graph shows the rate and depth of breathing in a person before exercise.

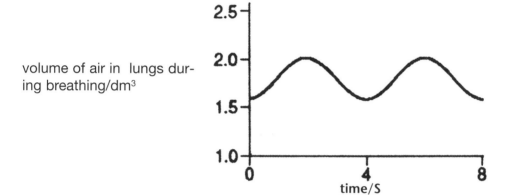

volume of air in lungs during breathing/dm^3

Which graph shows the rate and depth of breathing of the same person immediately after a period of exercise?

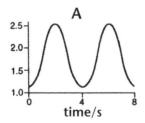

volume of air in lungs during breathing / dm^3

A

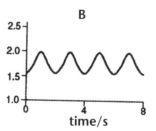

volume of air in lungs during breathing/dm^3

B

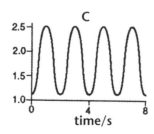

volume of air in lungs during breathing / dm^3

C

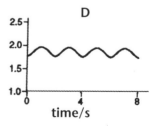

volume of air in lungs during breathing / dm^3

D

SECTION-B

1   List an **external** feature of each of the following types of organism that
    would identify the group to which it belongs.

Type of organism	Identifying feature
Arachnid	
Bird	
Insect	
Dicotyledonous plant	

[Total: 4]

2   **(a)** Describe in scientific terms the circulation of water in the environment.

....

....

....

....

.... [4]

(b) (i) Suggest how deforestation can affect the water cycle.

....

....

.... [2]

(ii) Describe **two** other effects of deforestation on the environment.

....

....

....

.... [2]

[Total: 8]

3 The graph shows changes in a population of small herbivores in a new habitat.

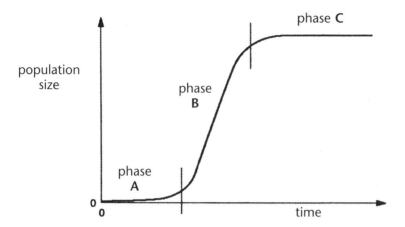

(a) (i) What name is used to describe this type of curve?

.... [1]

(ii) Complete the following table to link the named phases with those shown on the graph.

Name of phase	Phase on graph
log	
lag	
stationary	

[3]

(b) A breeding group of these herbivores was released into a second new habitat. This habitat had a much smaller food supply.

Suggest the effect this would have on the population graph for this second group.

....

....

....

....[2]

[Total:6]

4   The following figure shows a fetus developing in a uterus.

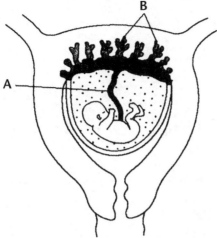

(a) (i) Name the part labelled **A**.

   A.. [1]

   (ii) What is unusual about the blood in the artery in **A** compared with the blood in most of the arteries in the mother?

   ....

   .... [1]

   (iii)The structures labelled **B** are called placental villi.

   Suggest **one** feature these might have that helps them to carry out their function efficiently.

   ....

   ....[1]

(b) The blood of the mother and the fetus do not normally mix.

   State two reasons why this is important.

   1 ....

   ....

   2 ....

   .... [2]

(c) The placenta is often described as the *'lung and kidney'* of the fetus.

   Explain why this is a good description.

   ....

....

....

.... [3]

[Total: 8]

5   (a)   The following figure shows a section through a seed of a dicotyledon.

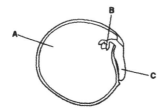

(i)   What is the role of part **A**?

.... [1]

(ii)   What do parts **B** and **C** of the seed develop into after germination?

B ....

C .... [2]

(b)   The following graph shows changes in mass of sets of pea seeds as they germinate and grow into seedlings. After germination, set **P** was grown in the dark and set **Q** in the light.

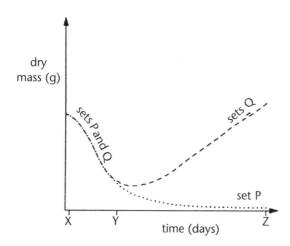

(i) Why is mass measured as dry mass?

....

.... [1]

(ii) Explain the changes in dry mass between days **X** and **Y** in both sets of seedlings.

....

....

....

....

.... [4]

(iii) Explain why there is a difference in the dry mass of sets **P** and **Q** between days **Y** and **Z**.

....

....

....

....

....

.... [4]

[Total: 12]

6 In cross 1, mice with black fur were bred with mice with white fur. All of their 16 offspring had black fur.

In cross 2, the offspring with black fur from cross 1 were interbred and produced 44 offspring of which 11 had white fur and the rest had black fur.

Using **B** and **b** to represent the two alleles controlling fur colour, complete the diagram, Fig. 6.1, to show the inheritance of fur colour in these two crosses.

cross 1

genotypes
of parents

mice with black fur | mice with white fur

genotypes
of gametes

genotypes
of offspring

phenotypes
of offspring

all with black fur

cross 2

genotypes of
offspring
from cross 1

genotypes
of gametes

genotypes
of offspring

phenotypes
of offspring   ___ ___ ___ ___

[Total: 6]

7   (a) Bile and lipase are concerned with the digestion of fats.

(i) Bile is made in the liver.

Where is lipase produced?

.... [1]

(II) Describe the role of these two substances in the process of fat
digestion.

....

....

....

....

....

.... **[4]**

(b) The products of digestion of carbohydrates, fat and proteins enter the blood.

    (i) Name the products of digestion that only enter the blood directly from the small intestine.

      ....

      .... **[2]**

    (II) Explain the roles of the liver in dealing with the products of digestion of carbohydrates and proteins.

      carbohydrates ....

      ....

      ....

      proteins ....

      ....

      .... **[4]**

[Total: 11]

8   The following figure shows a section through the heart.

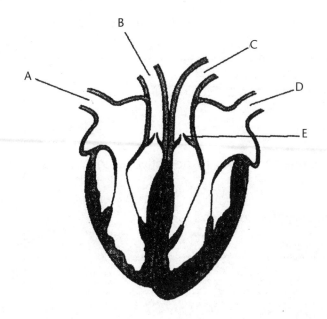

(a) (i) Name the two blood vessels **A** and **B**.

A ....

B .... **[2]**

(ii) Which of the blood vessels, **A**, **B**, **C** or **D**, carry oxygenated blood?

.... **[1]**

(iii) Name valve **E** and state its function.

name ....

function ....

.... **[2]**

(b) Some poor diets can increase the risk of a heart attack.

(i) Suggest two ways in which a poor diet could be changed to reduce the risk of heart attack.

1. ....

....

2. ....

.... **[2]**

(ii) Suggest two other factors, apart from diet, that could increase the risk of heart attack.

1. ....

....

2. ....

.... **[2]**

[Total: 9]

9 **(a)** Alcohol is described as a depressant and an addictive drug that can damage the body.

(i) State what is meant by each of the following terms:

depressant ....

....

addictive ....

.... **[2]**

(ii) State two long term effects that alcohol might have on the body.

1. ....

....

2. ....

.... **[2]**

(b) Suggest how alcohol might affect the performance of a car driver.

....

....

....

.... **[2]**

[Total: 6]

International General Certificate of Secondary Education

Model Test Paper II
BIOLOGY

M.M: 90   **Time: 1 hour 15 min**

SECTION-A

[Each question carries 1 mark]

1   Which of these describes excretion?

   A   getting rid of undigested food

   B   releasing energy from food

   C   removing waste products of metabolism

   D   transporting carbon dioxide in the blood

2   What happens to hormones and to urea in the liver?

	Hormones	**Urea**
A	broken down	broken down
B	formed	broken down
C	broken down	formed
D	formed	formed

3.   After a meal, the concentration of blood glucose increases.

Which organ removes this blood glucose and converts it into a storage compound?

   A   kidney

   B   liver

   C   pancreas

   D   rectum

4   The diagram shows shoots of maize seedlings.

Which shoot shows negative geotropism?

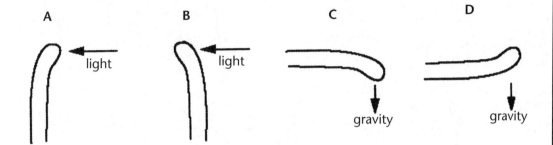

5   The diagram shows the male reproductive system.

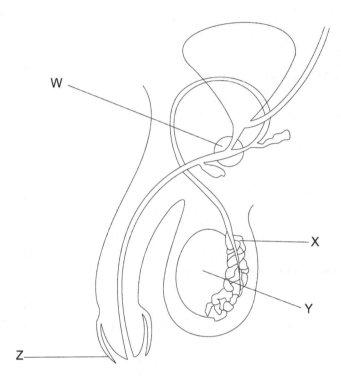

Where do sperm production, seminal fluid production and semen release occur?

	Sperm production	Seminal fluid production	Semen release
A	W	Y	X
B	X	Z	Y
C	Y	W	Z
D	Z	X	W

6 The diagram shows two flowers from the same plant.

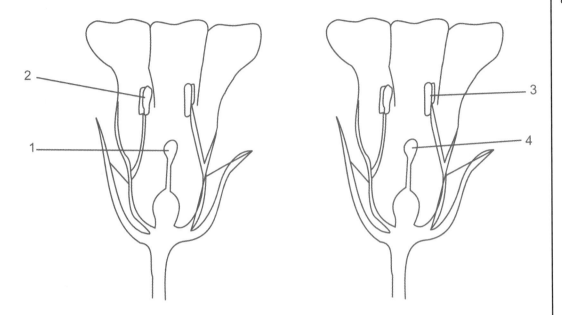

How can pollination occur between these two flowers?

	Pollen transferred from	Pollen transferred to
A	1	3
B	1	4
C	2	3
D	2	4

7 The diagram shows changes in the thickness of the uterus lining of a woman.

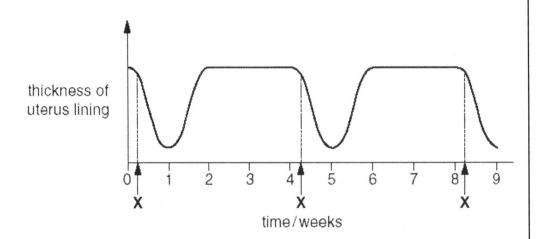

What happens each time at **X**?

A　fertilisation

B　implantation

C　menstruation

D　ovulation

8　By definition, what increases during growth?

A　complexity

B　dry mass

C　height

D　number of parts

9　The diagram shows the early growth of a green plant.

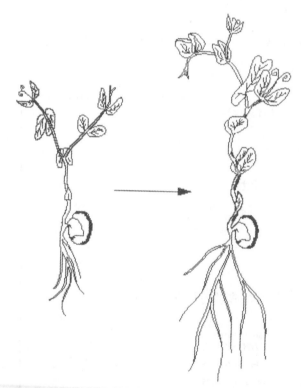

What is occurring?

	Mitosis	Development
A	✓	✓
B	✓	✗
C	✗	✓
D	✗	✗

key

✓ = occurs

✗ = does not occur

10 In the life cycle of a mammal, what describes the eggs or sperm and the cells of the embryo?

	Eggs or sperm	Cells of the embryo
A	diploid	diploid
B	diploid	haploid
C	haploid	diploid
D	haploid	haploid

11 What is **always** found in female gametes and **may** be found in male gametes?

A one X chromosome

B one Y chromosome

C two X chromosomes

D one X chromosome and one Y chromosome

12 In a species of plant, the allele for red flowers is dominant to the allele for white flowers.

Which offspring could result from a cross between a heterozygous red-flowered plant and a white-flowered plant?

A heterozygous red and homozygous red

B heterozygous red and homozygous white

C heterozygous red only

D homozygous white only

13 The diagram represents a pyramid of biomass within an ecosystem.

carnivores
herbivores
producers

Which shows the direction of energy flow through the pyramid?

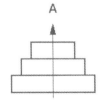 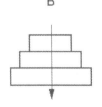 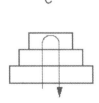 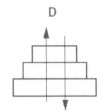

14 The diagram shows a food chain.

producers ⟶ herbivores ⟶ carnivores ⟶ top carnivores

trophic level: 1   2   3   4

If the carnivores in trophic level 3 suddenly die out as a result of disease, in which trophic levels will the number of organisms be likely to decrease?

A   1 and 2

B   1 and 4

C   2 only

D   2 and 4

15 Which process is **not** part of the carbon cycle?

A   combustion

B   photosynthesis

C   respiration

D   transpiration

16 The diagram shows the natural cycle of a substance.

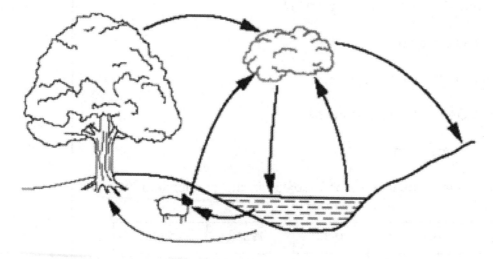

What is the substance?

A   carbon dioxide

B   nitrogen

C   oxygen

D   water

17 The graph shows the birth rate in a country.

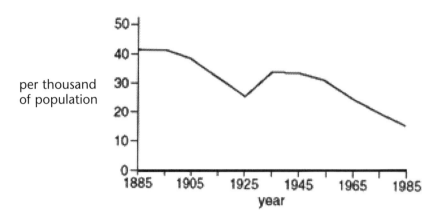

During which year is the population likely to be increasing at its lowest rate?

A 1885

B 1925

C 1935

D 1985

18 Why is it that pesticides sprayed in low concentrations may increase the yield of a crop, but may also be harmful to wildlife?

A pesticides cause acid rain

B pesticides enter the food chain

C pesticides increase the nitrates in soil

D pesticides kill other plants

19 The table shows the amount of carbon dioxide in the atmosphere in three different years.

Year	1930	1980	1990
carbon dioxide / parts per million	300	330	370

What is the most likely cause of this change?

A   destruction of rainforests

B   increased use of fertilisers containing nitrogen

C   pollution of air by sulphur dioxide

D   rise in the sea level

20 The diagram shows part of the water cycle.

At which stage does the use of nitrate fertilisers in agriculture cause the greatest pollution?

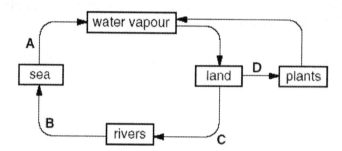

SECTION-B

1 Respiration is a characteristic of living organisms.

(a) State three other characteristics of living organisms.

1 ....

2 ....

3 .... **[3]**

(b) A remote control deep-sea probe collected mud from the seabed at a depth of 8000 m. The mud was thought to contain living microorganisms.

Suggest an investigation you might carry out which would indicate whether respiring microorganisms are present in a sample of the mud.

....

....

....

....

....

.... **[4]**

[Total: 7]

2 (a) The following figure shows a sugar cane flower that is wind pollinated.

(i) Name structures **X** and **Y**.

    X ....

    Y .... **[2]**

(ii) Explain how a feature, visible in the above figure, suggests that this flower is wind pollinated.

    ....

    ....

    .... **[2]**

(iii) Suggest two other features in which the sugar cane flower might be different from an insect-pollinated flower.

    1 ....

    2 .... **[2]**

(b) The following figure shows the dispersal of winged fruits around a tree in open grassland. Samples were taken along straight lines at 5 metre intervals.

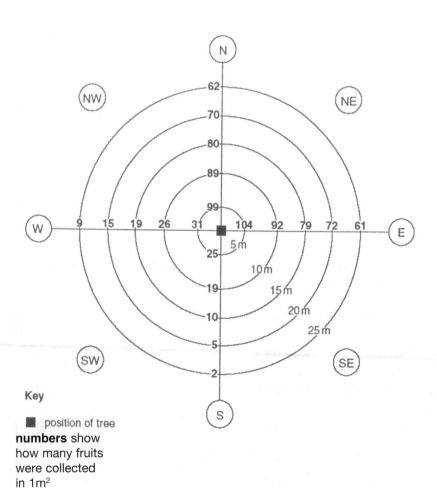

Key

■ position of tree
numbers show
how many fruits
were collected
in 1m²

(i) From which direction does the wind usually blow?

.... [1]

(ii) Explain how you arrived at your answer.

.... [1]

(iii) Suggest a reason, other than the wind, that might affect the distribution of these fruits.

....

.... [1]

[Total: 9]

3 The following figure shows the carbon cycle.

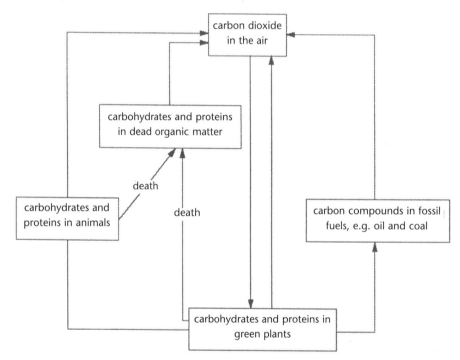

(a) Label one arrow in each case to show where each of the following processes occur in the carbon cycle.

(i) Combustion – using the letter **C** [1]

(ii) Decomposition – using the letter **D** [1]

(iii) Photosynthesis – using the letter **P** [1]

(iv) Respiration – using the letter **R** [1]

(b) Many environmentalists are concerned by the extent of deforestation that is happening throughout the world.

Suggest how deforestation might affect

(i) the carbon cycle;

....

....

.... **[2]**

(ii) the water cycle.

....

....

.... **[2]**

[Total: 8]

4 The following figure shows a typical animal cell and a typical plant cell.

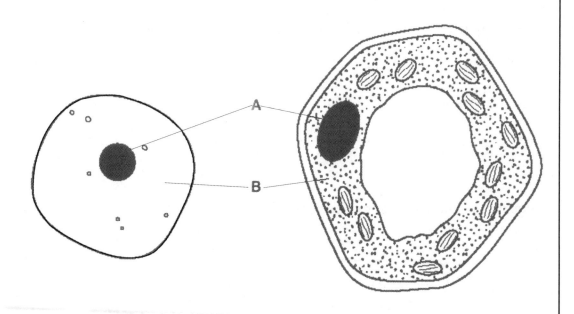

(a) (i) Name the parts of the cells labelled A and B.

A ....

B .... **[2]**

(ii) Label on the diagram, with a letter **C**, another structure that occurs in both cells. **[1]**

(b) For each of the following types of cell, state **one** way in which it is different from the animal cell in the above figure. State the function of each type of cell.

(i) Cell lining the trachea (windpipe)

difference ....

....

function ....

.... **[2]**

(ii) Red blood cell

difference ....

....

function ....

.... **[2]**

(c) Materials can enter the cells shown in the figure by diffusion and osmosis.

(i) Define diffusion.

....

....

.... **[2]**

(ii) Describe how osmosis differs from diffusion.

....

....

....

.... **[2]**

[Total: 11]

5 **(a)** Complete the following passage using **only** words from the list below.

diploid   gametes   haploid   meiosis   mitosis   red blood cells

The transfer of inherited characteristics to new cells and new individuals depends on two types of cell division.

During ...., the chromosomes are duplicated exactly and ....cells are produced.

However, during ...., the chromosome sets are first duplicated and then halved producing...................................cells. These cells will become... .   **[5]**

(b) Using a labelled, genetic diagram, explain the inheritance of the sex of an individual.   **[3]**

....

....

[Total: 8]

6 **(a)** Using a single line in each case, link each definition to the correct process.

Definition	Process
getting rid of fibre (roughage) from an animal	digestion
large food molecules broken down into simple substances	egestion
taking in food into an animal's alimentary canal	excretion
	ingestion

[3]

(b) Following figure shows the alimentary canal and associated organs.

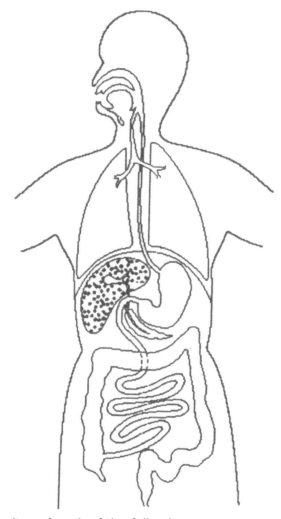

Label the sites of each of the following processes.

(i) absorption of water [1]

(ii) bile production [1]

(iii) glycogen storage [1]

(iv) lipase production [1]

[Total: 7]

7 Following figure shows the eye in section.

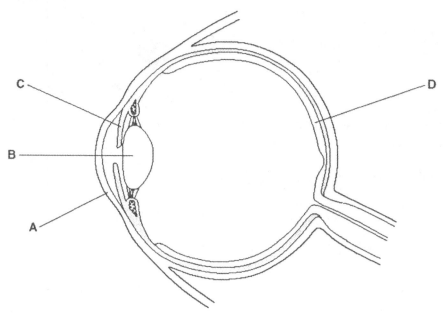

(a) State the function of each of the labelled parts of the eye.

A ....

....

B ....

....

C ....

....

D ....

.... **[4]**

(b) The following figure shows two external views of the eye.

changes
to

The change shown in the above figure happens when certain drugs are present in the blood.

Suggest how this could affect a person's vision.

....

....

....

.... **[2]**

[Total: 6]

8 **(a)** Translocation and transpiration are processes that occur in plants.

Describe each of these processes.

Translocation ....

....

....

....

Transpiration ....

....

....

.... **[4]**

(b) The following figure shows an investigation that was set up and left for 30 hours.

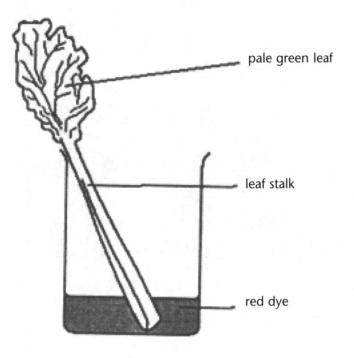

pale green leaf

leaf stalk

red dye

At the end of this time, the leaf had become red.

Suggest an explanation for this result.

....

....

....

....

....

.... **[5]**

[Total: 9]

9 The following figure shows some parts of an ecosystem.

zebra eats grass

(a) (i) In what form is energy passed from the Sun to the grass?

.... [1]

(ii) In what form is energy passed from the grass to the zebra?

.... [1]

(b) When the zebra dies, the energy in its body is released by decomposers.

(i) Name one group of microorganisms involved in this process.

.... [1]

(ii) Suggest in what form most of the energy is finally passed to the environment.

.... [1]

(c) Why is the movement of energy in an ecosystem described as a flow and not as a cycle?

....

.... [1]

[Total: 5]

SECTION-A

Question No.	Answer
1	A
2	B
3	Spider
4	B
5	C
6	D
7	D
8	B
9	A
10	D
11	B
12	D
13	B
14	C
15	B
16	A
17	A
18	C
19	B
20	C

SECTION-B

1

Arachnid	Body divided into two regions /4 pairs of legs
Bird	Presence of feathers and beak
Insect	Body divided into three regions/3 pairs of legs/two pairs of wings
Dicotyledonous plants	Leaf with mid rib/all the whorls of flower

2   Circulation of water
  • heat causes evaporation from water bodies
  • transpiration from plants
  • water vapours collect to form clouds
  • condensation of clouds due to cooling
  • falling of rain
  • the formation of water bodies again.

  (b) (i) Deforestation leads to decreased transpiration, less humidity and cloud formation, so less precipitation.
     (ii) Increased run off, increased flooding and erosion.

3 (a) (i) sigmoid

    (ii)

Name of phase	Phase on graph
Log	B
Lag	A
Stationary	C

(b) Stationary phase, population size does not go as high.

4. (a) (i) Umbilical cord
    (ii) Deoxygenated
    (iii) Rich blood supply

    (b) 1 Reduced risk of infections by pathogens,
        2 Maternal blood pressure too great for fetal vessels

    (c) Through the placenta oxygen is added to fetal blood, carbon dioxide is removed, urea is removed.

5. (a) (i) Nutrient store for seed.
    (ii) B grows to form the shoot system. C grows to form the root system.

    (b) (i) Not all water is from the living tissues

    (ii) Respiration occurs, food is broken down in to its components and used up, carbon dioxide is released in to the environment, so a drop in mass results.

    (iii) In set P only respiration is taking place but in set Q, since it is in the sunlight, photosynthesis is also taking place where food is produced and it is used for making more cells and so there is growth and dry mass will increase.

6. (i) Cross 1 BB, bb — genotype for parents
        B, b   — gametes
        ·Bb   genotype for the off-spring

    Cross 2 B & b, — genotype for the gametes
        BB, Bb & bb genotype of the offspring

7   (a) (i) Pancreas

    (ii) Bile emulsifies fats, neutralizes HCl in the stomach, raises pH levels, breaks down fats and converts them into fatty acids and glycerol.

    (b) (i) Glucose, amino acids.

    (ii) Convert glucose into glycogen for storage, break down amino acids to form urea.

8. (a) (i) A - Vena cava, B- Pulmonary artery
    (ii) Vessels C and D
    (iii) E - semilunar valve, Function - to prevent back flow of blood

    (b) (i) Reduce fat intake, increase fibre intake.
    (ii) Smoking, stress and tension, lack of exercise.

9. (i) Depressants are substances which decrease the speed of nerve impulses. The body demands more quantities of addictive substances.
    (ii) 1 Damage liver cells
        2 Increase of blood pressure.

    (b) It slows down the chemical reactions inside the body, reduces power of judgment, dizziness, driver may become more reckless, nausea.

Model Test Answers: Paper II

SECTION-A

Question No.	Answer
1	C
2	D
3	B
4	D
5	C
6	D
7	C
8	A
9	A
10	C
11	A
12	B
13	A
14	D
15	A
16	D
17	D
18	B
19	A
20	C

SECTION-B

1 (a) Excretion, growth, nutrition.
   (b) Put the mud in a muslin cloth, suspend over calcium hydroxide solution in a sealed container. Leave it for 12 hours. Lime water will turn milky if carbon dioxide is released as the process of respiration.

2 (a) (i)   X - stigma, Y - anther.
       (ii) feathery stigma, stamens hang outside of the flower.

       (iii) No smell or nectar, hairy pollen, small pollen grains.

   (b) (i)   South west
       (ii) Most of the fruits are found in the direction of north and east.
       (iii) Distribution of branches, density on the branches.

3. (a) Consult chapter 4, Nutrient cycle.

   (b) (i)   less leaves to photosynthesise, more carbon dioxide in the air, less leaves to decay and form humus.
       (ii) Less transpiration due to fewer numbers of leaves, less roots to absorb water, less water vapour in the air, so less rainfall

4. (a) (i)   A – Nucleus   B – Cytoplasm
       (ii) C – cytoplasm

   (b) (i)   cilia present only on the cell surface, function – to move mucus
       (ii) no nucleus, biconcave, contains haemoglobin, function – it carries oxygen.

   (c) (i)   movement of molecules down concentration gradient.
       (ii) Osmosis is the movement of water through a semipermeable membrane.

5. (a) mitosis, diploid, meiosis, haploid, gametes.
   (b) Consult chapter 3.

6. (a) top left _____ second right
       second left _____ top right
       bottom left _____ bottom right

   (b) (i) large intestine,
       (ii) liver
       (iii) liver
       (iv) pancreas

7 (a) A - lets light enter the eye
       B - focuses light to fall on the retina
       C - controls the amount of light entering
       D - changes light in to electrical impulses.

   (b) If too much light enters the retina, it causes blurred vision and can damage the retina.

8. (a) Translocation is the movement of soluble materials from the place of manufacturing to the place of necessity in the phloem.

   Transpiration is the loss of water vapour through the stomata into the atmosphere down the concentration gradient.

   (b) As leaves loose water by transpiration, water moves up the leaf through the xylem vessels.

9 (a) (i) sunlight
       (ii) chemical

   (b) (i) bacteria
       (ii) heat

   (c) energy is not passed back to the sun.

Index

A

absorption 63
acid rain 178, 180
active transport 43–4
adaptation 18–20, 22–24
adrenalin 101–2
agriculture 176
alcohol 112
alveoli 87
amphibians 11
antibodies 71, 78
arteries 72
auxin 98

B

bacteria 14, 17–8
   and nitrogen cycle 169
   see also microbes
binomial system 12
birds 26
blood and blood pressure 70–2, 74
bone 11, 50, 59
brain 34, 41, 102–3
breathing 85, 87, 113
breeding 141, 146, 167
brewing 83

C

capillaries 72, *72*, 73, *73*
carbohydrate 59
carbon dioxide 38, 73
   and breathing 86, 87
   and photosynthesis 52, 53
   and pollution 178, 182
cell 5, 25, 28, 31, 32, 36, 38, 40, 44
   specialisation 35
   and transport 38, 40, 44
   turgid 42, *42*
cellulose 31
central nervous system (CNS) 103
   see also nervous system

chlorophyll 31, 52
chloroplasts 31, 52, 56
chromosomes 31, 32, 141
   and genetic engineering 156
   and inheritance 143
circulation 72, 73, 74
classification 10–13, 15, 18–20, 25, 27
clones 149
community 162, 164, 183
competition 22, 23, 119, 120, 147
conservation 182
coordination 98
cytoplasm 31, 32

D

decomposers 164, 169, 181
deficiency disease 50, 58
deforestation 171, 176, 179
denitrifying bacteria 169
diabetics 109
dialysis 89, 91, 94
diet 58–9
diffusion 38, 43
digestion 61
disease 15, 20, 50, 58–9
DNA 31–2, 141, 144–5, 150–4
   and genetic engineering 156
double helix 145
drugs 60, 112

E

Earth Summit 182
ecosystems 166
effectors 143
energy 82, 162–5
enzymes 46–7
eutrophication 179
evolution 10, 12, 169
excretion 89
exercise 75, 77, 82, 84

extinction 166, 171, 182
eye 105

F

fats 48, 50
feeding *see* food
fermenters 48
fertilisers 178
fertility 136
fibre 59
fish 11, 26, 49, 59
flower 120–5
food 59, 64, 93
   genetically modified 156
   in insects 22, 22
   production 176–8
   tests 50, *50*
food chain 163–5
fungi 14, 18
   see also microbes

G

gametes 32, 148
genes 31, 148, 145
genetic engineering 146, 156, 157, 158
'genetic fingerprints' 157
genetics 117, 142, 155, 156, 157, 158
glucose 81, 82, 92, 113
   and photosynthesis 52, 56
glycogen 31, 109
greenhouse effect 178

H

habitat 182
haemoglobin 70
Harvey, William 72
health 6, 50, 132
heart 74, *74*, 75, 113
herbivores 162, 165, 169

Index